D0342185

Version 11

Supplement

MyFamily.com

© 2003

MINIMUM SYSTEM REQUIREMENTS

Family Tree Maker 11

- CPU: 166 MHz Pentium (300 MHz recommended).

- Operating System: Microsoft Windows 98/ME/XP Home Edition.

- RAM: 32 MB (64 MB recommended).

- Free Disk Space: 150 MB free hard disk space before installation.

- CD-ROM Drive: 2X CD-ROM drive or faster. This drive must be part of your system, as opposed to a drive that you access via a network.

Note: The CD-ROM drive does not need to be Kodak-compatible unless you want to insert Kodak Photo CD pictures into your Scrapbooks.

- Monitor: 640x480 display, 256 colors (or higher).

- Mouse: Microsoft compatible

- Internet Access: Required to access online data and features — minimum 28.8 Kbps connection speed.

Note: User is responsible for all Internet access fees and phone charges.

- Printer: Works with most popular printers (monochrome and color) supported by Windows.

- Optional Devices: Video capture board and sound board for video or audio clips. Scanner for digitizing graphic images. Digital camera. CD-R or CD-RW drive for backing up files to CD. Works with most popular CD-R/CD-RW drives.

- System requirements are based on requirements to run the Family Tree Maker program. User's Operating System requirements may be higher than those listed here. System configuration may require minor adjustments to the configurations of your operations system and/or updates to the hardware component drivers. As with all Windows programs, a faster processor, more RAM, and more free disk space will enhance performance.

Note: Only 50 MB of program files will be copied to your hard drive.

CONTENTS

WHAT'S NEW IN THIS VERSION

Family Tree Maker 11 is better than ever! Researching, organizing, and sharing your family history will be even easier with these powerful new features:

- **Back up Your File to CD** —Preserve your valuable family research when you back it up directly to a CD from Family Tree Maker. (Requires CD-R or CD-RW drive.) Works with most popular CD-R/CD-RW drives.

- **Streamlined Merge Process & Reports**— The easy new step-by-step process lets you merge individuals with complete control and precision.

- **Export Family Books as PDF files** — Save your Family Books in a PDF format to easily share your family story with others.

- **Add Notes to Family Books** — With a click of the mouse, you can customize your Family Books by adding a note on an individual or a marriage.

- **Preview Family Books** — See the contents and layout of your book before you print it. View formatted text, locations of pictures, backgrounds of trees, and more!

- **Family Books Tutorial** — Learn how to create, enhance, and share Family Books. You'll be creating professional-quality books in a matter of minutes for your whole family to enjoy.

- **Tabbed Preference Boxes** — Now it's easier than ever to set up Family Tree Maker with the tools and resources you need to organize, share, and preserve your family history.

- **Open Two Files Simultaneously** — Open, compare, and edit two Family Files at the same time. Perfect for checking a relative's genealogical research against your own files.

- **Copy and Paste** — Quickly and easily copy and paste a specific individual, entire branches, or complete trees from one file to another.

- **Export Reports to a Spreadsheet** — Print mailing lists, create a birthday calendar, organize medical information, and more!

- **Customize Your Background Color** — Customize Family Tree Maker by choosing your favorite color for the background of your Family Page.

- **Enhanced Help Instructions** — New step-by-step instructions in the Help file clearly explain how to use the features in Family Tree Maker.

INSTALLING THE SOFTWARE

To install Family Tree Maker:

1. Insert the Family Tree Maker Installation Program CD-ROM into your CD-ROM drive.

   Family Tree Maker may launch automatically. Simply follow the on-screen instructions to complete installation.

   If it does not, follow the remaining instructions below:

2. Click the Windows **Start** button and then select **Run**.

   Windows displays the **Run** dialog box.

3. Type "**D:SETUP**" and then click **OK**.

   Note: The "D" in "D:SETUP" stands for drive D. If you are installing from a CD-ROM drive other than drive D, type that letter instead. For example, to install from drive E, type **E:SETUP**.

4. Follow the on-screen instructions to complete the installation.

   During installation, you will see a dialog box titled "Select Optional Components." These items are *not required* to run Family Tree Maker and are made available as options, in case you wish to minimize the size of the installation. If you wish to use any of these components at a later time, you will be able to access/install them directly from the installation CD.

   Note: Please be sure to read the License Agreement during installation. If you need to refer to it in the future then open the file named license.txt in the same folder where you installed Family Tree Maker.

Technical Support

The Genealogy.com **Online Help Center** is a resource for answers to technical or customer service-related questions — 24 hours a day. Here you'll find easy-to-understand articles, tips, step-by-step instructions and tools for using Family Tree Maker. From the **Internet** menu, select **Technical Support**, or point your browser to **www.genealogy.com/help**.

If you prefer, you can write to: Genealogy.com, P.O. Box 990, Provo, UT 84059. Please be aware that the minimum response time for written communication is 4 to 6 weeks.

PROGRAM HELP IN FAMILY TREE MAKER

Remember, there is a convenient and easy-to-use Help program built into Family Tree Maker. It features a searchable Index of available help topics and instructions. You can open it anytime, from anywhere in the program.

> Just click the **F1** key. Or …

> From the **Help** menu, select **Search for help on…** to display the Help Topics dialog box.

Also, from the **Help** menu, you can select the **Genealogy "How-to" Guide** — your expert family history companion. Topics range from how to get started, whom to contact, and what to ask to overseas research tips, and more. Plus, built-in form letters and address directories make requesting official county records simple — just print and mail.

VIEWING FAMILY TREE MAKER 11 PDF MANUALS

The Family Tree Maker 11 Getting Started Manual and QuickStart Guide in PDF format are included on the Family Tree Maker 11 Installation CD and are automatically installed in the same folder where you installed Family Tree Maker. To view your PDF manuals, you will need the Adobe Acrobat Reader. This program may already be installed in your system. If not:

1. Go to **www.adobe.com**.

2. Download the free Acrobat Reader and follow their instructions to install it on your system. The program will launch automatically when you click on any PDF file.

To find and read your manuals:

You'll find the Getting Started Manual, Quick Start Manual, and Readme file on your computer. Inside the Family Tree Maker folder, open the Manuals folder.

To view your PDF manuals, you will need the Adobe Acrobat Reader, a free program that may already be installed on your system.

To open files in PDF format, double-click on the icon. Adobe Acrobat Reader will launch automatically and open the file.

If the file does not open, you may not have Adobe Acrobat Reader. To download it, do the following:

1. Go to the Adobe website.

2. Download the Reader and follow the instructions to install it on your system.

3. Once it is installed, you can now double click on your PDF manual to view it.

For additional assistance, go to the Help section within Adobe Acrobat Reader or visit our Online Help Center.

Once Adobe Acrobat Reader is installed, open the folder. You can now double-click on your PDF manual to view it. You can view the manuals from the CD, save them to your hard drive, or print them out for easy reference.

For additional assistance, go to the Help section within Family Tree Maker or visit our Online Help Center at **www.genealogy.com/help**.

BACK-UP YOUR FILE TO CD

Create a backup copy of your Family File and save it to a CD. Don't let viruses, hard drive crashes, or corrupted floppy disks ruin your valuable family research. Gone are the days needing multiple floppy disks to back-up your large Family Files. Now you can quickly and easily back-up your Family File directly from the program to a single CD. (Requires CD-R or CD-RW drive.)

Store the CD with your family history data at an offsite location to protect the information in case of fire or flood, or share your Family File with friends and family members with Family Tree Maker. Should you ever need to restore your file from the CD, you can accomplish this in just a matter of seconds.

To manually back up your Family File to a CD:

1. From the **File** menu, select **Backup Family File** (ALT, F, B).

2. Select the **Writable CD Drive** option.

3. After making your selection, click **OK** or press **Enter**.

   The first time you are backing up your file to a CD-ROM, you may get a message asking you to install a driver by clicking OK. This message will appear only once.

   > **Note:** Family Tree Maker supports most popular CD-R/CD-RW drives. For additional compatibility information, please go to the Genealogy.com **Online Help Center.** From the Internet menu, select **Technical Support**, or point your browser to **www.genealogy.com/help**.

STREAMLINED MERGE PROCESS

Merging and appending data from one Family File to another has never been easier! Family Tree Maker 11's new merge process clearly and effectively walks you through the few simple steps needed to complete a merge.

With Family Tree Maker 11, you'll receive a complete list of all Likely Matches and then have the ability to select the appropriate individuals to merge.

If only one file has information on the individual, then those facts are included in the merge. If both files have facts, only those in the destination file are kept. You will always be alerted when this conflict arises.

In addition, the Merge Reports have been reformatted and simplified with new column headers and explanations. You'll be able to clearly and effectively view the details of your pending or completed merge. Merge reports contain new column headers and explanations to help you clearly view and understand which individuals and sources have been merged, appended, or remained unchanged due to the merge.

ENHANCED FAMILY BOOKS

Family Tree Maker 11 includes powerful new features to make your Family Books easier to create, more informative, more attractive, and easier to share with your friends and relatives.

Export Family Books as PDF Files

The ability to export trees and reports to a PDF format has now been extended to include Family Books. By saving your Family Book as a PDF file, you can preserve and share your family history more easily and present it exactly as you intended.

In addition, you can upload the PDF file to your family home page or send it to relatives via e-mail. Sharing your research is simple and economical since you don't have to print, copy, and collate books, or ship bulky and expensive packages. No matter where your family and friends are located, they'll have fast and easy access to a Family Book that you created.

Adobe's PDF (Portable Document Format) is a universal file format — a convenient way to prepare documents for uploading to a Web site, sending through e-mail, or printing at a service bureau. Anyone with Adobe Acrobat Reader (a free program) can read or print out the document. Best of all, the document will look the same, no matter what kind of computer the recipient has.

To export your Family Book in PDF format:

1. In the Book View, select the **Export Book** command (ALT, F, E) from the File menu, and choose **To Acrobat (PDF)**.

2. Select the destination for your exported file. Unless you specify otherwise, the file will be saved to the directory where the current family file is saved or to the location where you most recently saved a file during this session.

3. Click **OK** or press **Enter**. Your file is saved.

The first time you create a PDF, the following message appears:

To view an exported PDF file, you will need the Adobe Acrobat PDF viewer. This may already be installed on your system. If not, it is available at www.adobe.com.

Add Notes to Family Books

Preserve and share the fascinating details of your family history by adding notes on an individual or a marriage. You no longer need to copy the contents of a note and paste them in a text item in your Family Book. Notes now appear in the Available items list in the Book View, and can be added to your book with a simple click of the mouse.

There are two ways to add Notes to your book.

To add Notes to your book using drag-and-drop:

1. From the Available items list on the left, select the Note you wish to add by clicking on it.

2. Continuing to hold down the mouse button, drag the Note to the Outline list on the right.

3. Release the mouse button when the Note entry is where you want it to appear in the finished book. Family Tree Maker adds the item.

4. To move the Note up or down the list, select it and drag it to a new place.

To add Notes to your book using buttons:

1. Select the Note you want to add from the Available items list on the left by clicking on the Note.

2. Click **Add.**

3. Family Tree Maker adds the note you selected to the bottom of the Outline list on the right (directly above the Index if you have one).

4. To move it up or down the list, select the item to be moved from the Outline list on the right, then click **Move up** or **Move down.**

   All text formatting from the Notes section is kept when you transfer notes to your book.

Family Book Preview

See exactly what your Family Book will look like as you create it. Quickly view your entire book — formatted notes, pictures, trees, reports, and more! Use the Book Preview button to display a complete layout of your book before you print it.

To preview your Family Book:

1. From the Book View, click the **Preview Book button**.

2. Family Tree Maker automatically converts your book to a PDF format and opens it in Adobe Acrobat Reader.

Family Books Tutorial

The Family Books Tutorial illustrates how to create, enhance and share Family Books. You'll be creating professional-quality books in a matter of minutes for your whole family to enjoy for generations to come.

To view the Family Books Tutorial:

1. Make sure you are connected to the Internet.

2. From the **Help** menu in Family Tree Maker, select **Books Tutorial**.

TABBED PREFERENCE BOXES

Easily customize your copy of Family Tree Maker through the new Tabbed Preference dialog box. Now it is simple to navigate through the many preferences to set up Family Tree Maker with the tools and resources you need to better organize, share, and preserve your family history.

To set your preferences:

1. From the **File** menu, select **Preferences**.

2. Then, make your selection from each tab, as listed below.

3. When you have finished with one tab, click the next.

   The following settings are available through the Tabbed Preferences.

   ### Editing

   Allows you to choose between Insert and Overwrite typing modes.

   Allows you to select error checking during data entry. Family Tree Maker can automatically check the information that you enter in the Family Page for name errors and unlikely birth, marriage, and death dates, misspellings, and other types of errors.

   Allows you to choose Spell Check options from these: Ignore known names, Ignore capitalized words, and Ignore words with numbers.

   Allows you to choose which fields in Family Tree Maker act as Fastfields.

   ### Dates & Measures

   Lets you choose between using English and metric units of measure, and select the default date format, style, and label.

   ### File Protection & Backup

   Allows you to choose backup and overwrite-protection options.

   ### Help & Setup

   Allows you to choose background color for the Family Page.

   Allows you to choose in which views Cue Cards and Bubble Help windows appear with helpful tips and information.

Allows you to choose whether to sort the More About Facts page by fact name or by date.

Allows you to choose the buttons that appear on the Family Tree Maker toolbar.

Allows you to choose whether to go to the Individual Facts Card dialog box (default) or Family Page when clicking an individual in trees and reports.

Allows you to choose FamilyFinder and CD Search options, including whether or not to expand your name searches to include names that sound alike but are not spelled exactly like the name for which you are searching. (Soundex)

Labels, Titles, & LDS tab

Allows you to globally change field labels, select default titles (such as "Mr." and "Mrs.") to use with all of the individuals in your Family File, and choose compliance with LDS formatting in Family Tree Maker.

Picture Quality

Allows you to choose default compression and resolution levels for any future pictures that you import into Scrapbooks.

Reference Numbers

Displays a dialog box where you can activate automatic reference numbers and customize the number format.

4. When you have made all your selections, click **OK** or press **Enter**.

    Note: Some changes will not take effect until the next time you start Family Tree Maker.

OPEN TWO FILES SIMULTANEOUSLY

Now you can open, compare, and edit two Family Files at the same time. This new feature is perfect for checking a relative's genealogical research against your own files or for going through pedigrees downloaded from the World Family Tree.

To open a second file:

1. From the File menu, select **Open**.

2. Select the file you want. Click **OK** or press **Enter**.

If you attempt to open a third file, you will be prompted to close the file you are currently working in. All changes will be saved.

> **Note**: Changes made to the Preferences settings may not be applied immediately to two opened files. We recommend that you close and re-open files after making changes to the Preference settings.

COPY AND PASTE BETWEEN TWO FILES

Quickly and easily copy and paste a specific individual, entire branches, or complete trees from one file to another. Copy and paste a specific individual, and individual's descendants and ancestors, or all the individuals in a tree from one file to another.

To copy and paste between files:

1. Open two files in Family Tree Maker.

2. Go to a Family Page, tree, or report that contains the individual you want to copy.

3. Select the individual whose information you want to copy to another tree by clicking on their name in the source file.

   Note: It's best to choose an individual who already exists in the destination file. For example, if you want to add your grandfather's ancestors to your family tree, select your grandfather in the source file.

4. Click **File** and select **Copy.**

5. From the flyout menu, select **Copy Selected Individual, Copy All Individuals in [name of view], Copy Individual & All Ancestors,** or **Copy Individual & All Descendants.**

6. In the destination file, click on the location in a Family Page, tree, or report where you want to add the new individual or branch. If the location is occupied, the two individuals will be merged with your approval. Additional individuals copied will be appropriately merged or appended.

Troubleshooting

To Undo Paste Individuals:

1. Click **Edit** and select **Undo.**

2. Click **Yes** to revert to the file as it was before you pasted.

Note: Information not copied includes Family Books and Saved Views. In addition marriage items are not copied if only one of the partners is included in the copy.

If you cannot see the new individuals, make sure you are in the correct view. You will be able to see only the individuals who belong in the current view. For example, if you have pasted in a line of descendants, they will not show up on the Ancestor tree. Change views to see the new individuals in their proper place on your family tree.

If you want to add a line that is not represented in your original tree, you have two options.

Create the new individual in the proper place in the destination file. You don't need to fill in all the details. Or you can open the Family Page in the destination file and paste into an empty parent or child location.

EXPORT REPORTS TO A SPREADSHEET FORMAT

Print mailing lists, create a birthday calendar, organize medical information, and more! It's easy with this new feature, which combines the information already entered in Family Tree Maker with the power of spreadsheet applications, such as Microsoft Excel.

To export a report to a spreadsheet:

1. From the appropriate report view, go to the **File** menu and select **Export** Report (ALT, F, E). Depending on the view, it will give you the option to Export to PDF or Export To Acrobat, Plain Text, Word Processor, or Spreadsheet.

   Note: Select **Export Report** from the **File** menu. Do not select **Copy/Export Family File**. Only select reports can be exported to CSV format.

2. Use the Save as Type drop-down menu to select **To Spreadsheet (CSV).**

3. Select the destination for your exported file and click OK. Make a note of where you are saving the exported file.

4. Your report is saved in a CSV format. You can now open it from your spreadsheet program.

CUSTOMIZE YOUR BACKGROUND COLOR

Now you can customize Family Tree Maker with a variety of colors, from pale blue to light green, including rose, magenta, gold, and more. Choose a color to match your family crest, clan tartan, or childhood home.

How to select a custom background color:

1. From the **File** menu, select **Preferences**.

2. The Tabbed Preferences dialog box will appear. Click **Help & Setup.**

3. Choose your background color from the dropdown menu.

3. Click **OK** or press **Enter**. Changes will take effect next time you start Family Tree Maker.

TUTORIALS AND ENHANCED HELP INSTRUCTIONS

Family Tree Maker is now easier to use than ever! Improved step-by-step help instructions and multimedia tutorials help you to get started using Family Tree Maker and introduce you to the major features of the program. The new Help Tutorials visually walk you through the few simple steps needed to get started using Family Tree Maker and to create Family Books. Whether you are a novice or have years of experience, these tutorials offer useful tips for gathering and preserving your family heritage with Family Tree Maker.

The **Getting Started Tutorial** takes you step-by-step through the process of recording your family history with Family Tree Maker.

To access the Getting Started Tutorial:

1. From the Family Tree Maker **Help** menu, select **Getting Started.**

2. The tutorial will begin playing.

In addition, Family Tree Maker continues to include a Getting Started Manual in PDF format within the installation CD-ROM for quick reference. See pages 5 and 6 of this supplement for instructions.

Our multimedia **Genealogy Tutorial** gives you a complete introduction to the types of records that will help you trace your family history and tips on where to locate those records.

To access the Genealogy Tutorial:

1. Insert the Family Tree Maker installation CD into your computer's CD drive.

2. From the **Help** menu within Family Tree Maker, select **Learn About Genealogical Records.**

3. The tutorial will begin.

The **Family Books Tutorial** is available online to help you create heirloom-quality books for your own family story.

To access the Family Books Tutorial:

1. From the Family Tree Maker **Help** menu, select **Books Tutorial.**

    Note: Make sure your computer is ready to access the Internet.

2. Your Internet Browser will open and go to the first page of the tutorial.

3. The tutorial will begin playing.

Thank you for purchasing Family Tree Maker 11. We know you'll enjoy all the new features included in this version. Be sure to visit **www.Genealogy.com** to search for your ancestors through census, passenger, and vital records, plus much more!

The Official
Family Tree Maker®
Version 10
fast&easy

Rhonda McClure

Premier

Press

Most of the time, our books are copyright Premier Press. Occasionally, the copyright belongs to the author. Please do not assume that what is printed here is correct. Double-check the copyright with the acquisitions editor.

The Premier Press logo and related trade dress are trademarks of Premier Press, Inc. and may not be used without written permission.

Publisher: Stacy L. Hiquet
Marketing Manager: Heather Hurley
Senior Acquisitions Editor: Emi Smith
Project Editor/Copy Editor: Fran Hatton
Editorial Assistants: Margaret Bauer, Elizabeth Barrett
Technical Reviewer: Amy Johnson Crow
Interior Layout: Danielle Foster
Cover Designer: Mike Tanamachi
Indexer: Sharon Shock
Proofreader: Sara Gullion

Family Tree Maker is a registered trademark of Genealogy.com, LLC a subsidiary of A&E Television Networks. World Family Tree, InterneTree, Family Finder, and Family Archives are trademarks of Genealogy.com, LLC. All other trademarks are the property of their respective owners. All other trademarks are the property of their respective owners.

Important: Premier Press cannot provide software support. Please contact the appropriate software manufacturer's technical support line or Web site for assistance.

Premier Press and the author have attempted throughout this book to distinguish proprietary trademarks from descriptive terms by following the capitalization style used by the manufacturer.

Information contained in this book has been obtained by Premier Press from sources believed to be reliable. However, because of the possibility of human or mechanical error by our sources, Premier Press, or others, the Publisher does not guarantee the accuracy, adequacy, or completeness of any information and is not responsible for any errors or omissions or the results obtained from use of such information. Readers should be particularly aware of the fact that the Internet is an ever-changing entity. Some facts may have changed since this book went to press.

ISBN: 1-59200-035-5

Library of Congress Catalog Card Number: 2002108328

Printed in the United States of America

02 03 04 05 BH 10 9 8 7 6 5 4 3 2 1

Premier Press, a division of Course Technology
2645 Erie Avenue, Suite 41
Cincinnati, Ohio 45208

For Rhody and Carnie, I love you both

Acknowledgments

A book is a group effort. While the author comes up with the original concept and begins to bring that concept to life, there are many others who help along the way before that book becomes a finished project. Without the help and input of these others, this book would not be the work you are holding today. To Emi Smith, thank you for the chance to work with you and Premier Press again. Thanks to Fran Hatton, her input throughout the book is appreciated. Special thanks to Amy Johnson Crow for her willingness to act as tech editor. Finally particular thanks to Brian Bond of Genealogy.com who always is there when I need him to answer questions or offer insight into the program.

About the Author

RHONDA R. McCLURE has managed to combine the best of both worlds—computers and genealogy. She has been using a computer to aid in her genealogical research since 1985. She has been teaching genealogists for more than 10 years on the benefits of their genealogy software; a time-saving addition to their research when understood. She can be found at national conferences guiding genealogists to an understanding of Family Tree Maker and other genealogy subjects. This is her third *Fast & Easy* book for Premier Press, she was the author for *Family Tree Maker 8 Fast & Easy* in 2000 and the *The Official Family Tree Maker Version 9 Fast & Easy* in 2001.

Contents at a Glance

Contents

PART III
WORKING IN FAMILY TREE MAKER 127

PART IV
GETTING TO KNOW FAMILY TREE MAKER
TREES AND REPORTS 179

PART VI
ADVANCED FAMILY TREE MAKER METHODS 297

Introduction

This *Fast & Easy* book from Premier Press will help you learn Family Tree Maker 10 quickly, leaving you more time for researching your family history and requiring less time for learning how to enter it into a program. Family Tree Maker is a multifaceted program able not only to track your ancestry, but also to produce beautiful reports and books when you wish to share what you have found. Even if you have never used a genealogy program before, you will find that Family Tree Maker's interface and options make it possible to keep track of even the most tangled of family trees. With the capability to include digitized images, Family Tree Maker gives you the opportunity to share more than just names, dates, and places. This book introduces you to many of the features available in Family Tree Maker so you can enjoy this hobby you've discovered. If you have used Family Tree Maker before, you may find some new tricks in the Advanced Methods section.

Who Should Read This Book?

This book is written with the novice computer user in mind. In it, you are taken on a hands-on trip through the Family Tree Maker program. The many illustrations let you check your progress as you master each new feature or process. Even if you are familiar with computers, though, you may have only recently been introduced to Family Tree Maker. In either case, this book offers you an easy-to-follow tour of the program and all that you can accomplish. Comparing your own screen to the screen captures in the book allow you to easily see if you are using the program correctly. Finally, those who feel comfortable with the basic features of Family Tree Maker may find some shortcuts or new methods for working with the program, especially in the Advanced Methods section.

This book is organized by tasks. Some tasks may require many steps, and others may branch off into enhancements or additional features. A quick perusal of the Table of Contents should lead you right to the process you are trying to accomplish. Then it is just a matter of reading through the steps.

Special Features of This Book

As you work with this book, you will discover that the emphasis is on tasks. This is by design, so that you can master what you need in an easy-to-follow format. There are a couple of features, though, that will supply you with additional information as you work with the Family Tree Maker program.

TIP

Tips offer you useful hints about features in Family Tree Maker that can speed up the task at hand or enhance your report output.

NOTE

Notes offer additional information about Family Tree Maker or about genealogy and sharing your family tree.

In the appendixes you will find help for installing the Family Tree Maker software and useful tables of keyboard shortcuts to make your data entry speedier.

Happy family tree climbing!

PART I

Introduction to Family Tree Maker

1

Getting Started with Family Tree Maker

Before you can take advantage of the many features of this program, you must first know how to launch or open it. You must then have some information about your family history to enter into it. Family Tree Maker offers different methods for both opening the program and beginning a new Family File. In this chapter, you'll learn how to:

- Start Family Tree Maker using the menu
- Start Family Tree Maker using the desktop icon
- Enter information using the Family Tree Maker wizard
- Begin your Family File using the Family Page

Starting Family Tree Maker

Before you can enter your family history data into Family Tree Maker, you must be able to launch the program. When you installed Family Tree Maker (see Appendix A, "Installing Family Tree Maker"), the installation set up two different ways for you to launch the Family Tree Maker program.

Launching Family Tree Maker from the Menu

For each program installed on your computer, there is a Start Menu option that allows you to launch the program. Family Tree Maker is no different.

1. **Click** on the **Start button** on the Windows Taskbar. The Start menu will appear.

2. **Move** the **mouse pointer** to All Programs. The menu for all programs will appear.

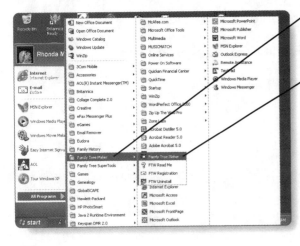

3. **Move** the **mouse pointer** to **Family Tree Maker**. The Family Tree Maker menu will appear.

4. **Click** on **Family Tree Maker**. Family Tree Maker will start.

Launching Family Tree Maker from the Desktop

Family Tree Maker installs an icon on the Windows desktop that saves you time and steps by taking you directly to the Family Tree Maker program.

1. **Double-click** on the **Family Tree Maker icon**. Family Tree Maker will start.

> ### NOTE
>
> The desktop in Windows is the main screen you see when you first boot up your computer. This screen has icons for different programs you have installed as well as other items that were installed by Windows the first time you turned on the computer.

Creating a New Family File

The first step to using Family Tree Maker is to enter information about your family. For most of us, this means taking the bits and pieces shared by family members and entering them into the program.

Using the Family Tree Maker Wizard

Family Tree Maker offers an easy introduction to help you enter data about yourself and your family. As soon as Family Tree Maker opens and you have named your family file, a wizard appears to help you enter information.

> ### NOTE
>
> Family Tree Maker will prompt you for a file name for your new Family File. After you type a file name in the File name field, just click on the Save button.

TIP

Family Tree Maker defaults to the "My Documents" folder on your computer when saving this first family file. You can use the Save in down arrow to select any folder you wish on your system.

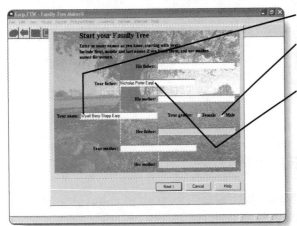

1. **Type** your **name** in the Your name field.

2. **Click** on the appropriate **gender radio button**. The gender will be selected.

3. **Click** in the **Your father field** and **enter** your **father's name**.

TIP

When using the Start Your Family Tree wizard, you must enter at least three names, usually yours and your parents'.

NOTE

To find out how to bypass the wizard, please see the next section, "Beginning Directly in the Family Page."

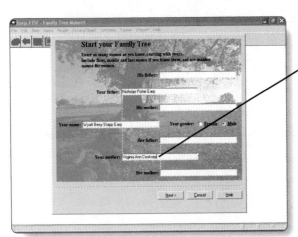

4. **Press** the **Tab key**. The cursor will move to the Your mother field.

5. **Type** your **mother's name** in the Your mother field.

6. **Press** the **Tab key**. The cursor will move to the His father field.

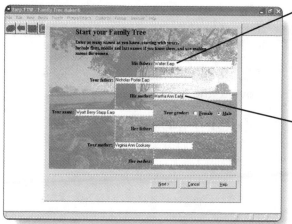

7. **Type** the **name** of your father's father (your paternal grandfather) in the His father field.

8. **Press** the **Tab key.** The cursor will move to the His mother field.

9. **Type** the **name** of your father's mother (your paternal grandmother) in the His mother field.

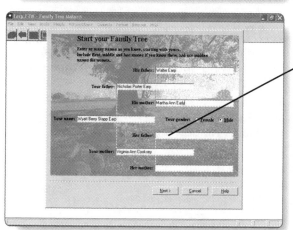

10. **Press** the **Tab key**. The cursor will move to the Her father field.

11. **Type** the **name** of your mother's father (your maternal grandfather) in the Her father field.

12. **Press** the **Tab key.** The cursor will move to the Her mother field.

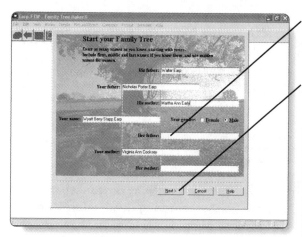

13. **Type** the **name** of your mother's mother (your maternal grandmother) in the Her mother field.

14. **Click** on the **Next button**. The Births screen will appear.

NOTE

Don't worry if you don't know all this information. Fill in as much as you can so that you have some information to work with.

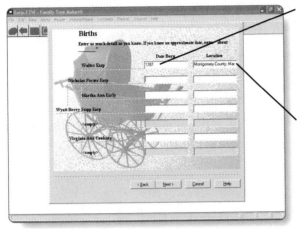

15. In the Date Born field, **enter** the **date of birth** for the first person in the Births window.

16. **Press** the **Tab key**. The cursor will move to the Location field.

17. **Type** the **place of birth** for that person.

18. **Press** the **Tab key** to work through the remaining individuals in the Births screen and **enter** any known **birthplaces and dates of birth**.

19. **Click** on the **Next button**. The Deaths window will appear.

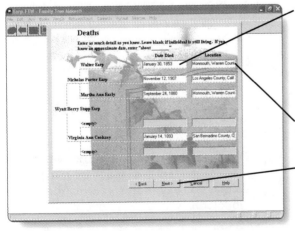

20. In the Date Died field, **type** the **date of death** for the first person in the Deaths window.

21. **Press** the **Tab key**. The cursor will move to the Location field.

22. **Enter** the **place of death** for that person.

23. **Click** on the **Next button** when you have finished entering death information for those people on whom you have death dates or places. The FamilyFinder Search window will appear.

24. **Click** on the **Skip Search**. The option will be selected.

25. **Click** on the **Finish button**. A Family Tree Maker message box will appear, telling you that you can run a search any time by clicking on the FamilyFinder icon.

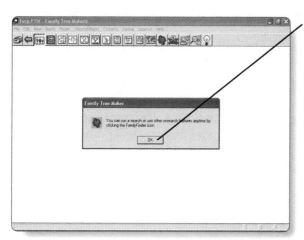

26. **Click** on **OK**. The message box will disappear.

NOTE

You will be introduced to the FamilyFinder search and report tool in Chapter 10, "Searching Your Family Tree File."

TIP

If the Cue Card appears, press the Escape key or click on OK to close it. For more information on the Cue Card, see Chapter 2, "Understanding Family Tree Maker."

Beginning Directly in the Family Page

While the wizard guides you through the initial entry of the basic information about yourself and some immediate family members, you might wish to bypass it and begin entering information directly into the Family Page in Family Tree Maker.

1. **Click** on the **Cancel button**. A message box will appear, asking you whether you want to go to the Family Page.

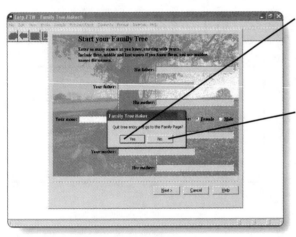

2a. **Click** on **Yes**. The message box will disappear and you will go directly to the Family Page.

OR

2b. **Click** on **No**. The message box will disappear and you will go back to the wizard.

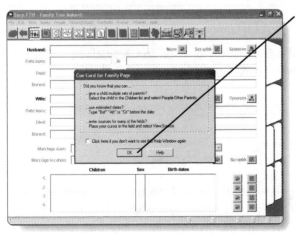

3. **Click** on **OK** in the Cue Card. The Cue Card will disappear.

NOTE

See Chapter 3, "Family Tree Maker for Beginners," for information on how to enter information in the empty Family Page.

Building from Another Person's Research

You may be one of those fortunate enough to have family members who have already been researching the family tree. If they are willing to share, ask them to send you a GEDCOM (GEnealogical Data COMmunication) file. Family Tree Maker can import this file into your Family File. See Chapter 21, "Working with GEDCOM Files and Other Family Files," for more information.

2

Understanding Family Tree Maker

Learning any new program requires an introduction to the program's interface. There are usually some new menu items, push buttons, and choices that are specific to the program. This is true of Family Tree Maker, and this chapter introduces you to those items. In this chapter, you'll learn how to:

- Execute commands with menus and toolbars
- Use dialog boxes and scroll bars
- Navigate the various Family Page fields
- Select different views
- Move information
- Exit Family Tree Maker

Exploring Family Tree Maker

When you look at the Family Tree Maker screen, you will see a number of menus, buttons and tabs. These buttons allow you to perform the different tasks in the program. The tabs allow you to maneuver through your family history database. This section introduces you to these features.

Using Menus

Menus are lists of the functions built into software programs. The Family Tree Maker menus are activated by clicking on the words that appear along the top bar of the Family Tree Maker program. Each menu contains a list of related commands.

1. **Click** on a **menu** name. The menu you chose will appear.

NOTE

If a menu command is followed by a right-pointing arrow, another menu will appear when you move the mouse pointer to that menu option. If a menu command is grayed out, it means that the command is not currently available. You might need to perform some other action in order to activate the grayed-out command.

TIP

Some menu commands have keyboard shortcuts. You will find the keyboard shortcuts listed to the right of the menu command. You can use these shortcuts to execute commands, rather than using the menus. To learn about some of the most popular keyboard shortcuts, see Appendix B, "Using Keyboard Shortcuts."

2. **Move** the **mouse pointer** over a menu item with a right-pointing arrow. A second menu will appear.

3. **Move** the **mouse pointer** over an option on the second menu. The menu item will be highlighted.

NOTE

Click on a menu option to execute that command. This might change the view of the screen, open a dialog box requesting additional information or choices, or open another window.

Using Toolbars

There is one toolbar in Family Tree Maker. The toolbar offers buttons to access some of the more popular views, as well as a few shortcut buttons to some of the unique commands.

1. **Move** the **mouse pointer** over each of the toolbar buttons. A tip describing the function of that toolbar button will appear.

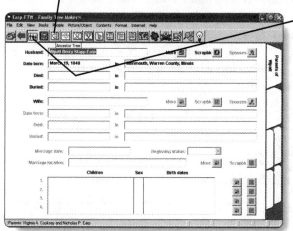

2. **Click** on the **Family Page button** on the toolbar. The Family Page window will appear.

NOTE

When you click on the various toolbar buttons or make certain menu choices, Family Tree Maker will open a Cue Card. The Cue Card offers some tips for working with that option.

TIP

If you do not wish to see the Cue Cards, you can turn them off. Click on the Click here if you don't want to see this Help Window again check box, then click on the OK button. To learn more about turning this feature on and off, see Chapter 23, "Working with System Preferences."

Understanding Dialog Boxes

In Family Tree Maker, dialog boxes allow you to make choices and select additional options. They also allow you to select items or preferences. Before you work with the example in this section, be sure you are in the Family Page, which is the default screen in Family Tree Maker, and that you're working with a family that has both a husband and a wife.

1. Click on the **People menu**. The menu will appear.

2. Click on **Other Spouses**. The Other Spouses dialog box will open.

TIP

You can also access the Other Spouses dialog box by pressing the F3 key.

Moving around with Scroll Bars

In Family Tree Maker, scroll bars are found to the right of and at the bottom of windows, where the text or report extends beyond the limits of the window. There are four different ways to move up and down or sideways using the scroll bars.

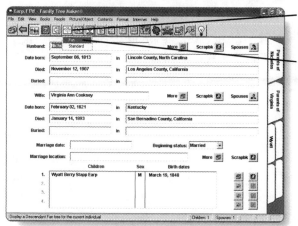

1. Click on the **Descendant Tree button**. The Descendant Tree menu will appear.

2. Click on **Fan**. The Descendant Fan Tree window will appear.

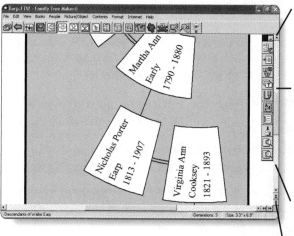

• **Click** on the **arrow** at either end of the vertical (or horizontal) scroll bar. This will scroll the page up or down (or side to side) one line at a time.

• **Press and hold** the **mouse button** on the vertical (or horizontal) scroll box and **drag** the **scroll box** up or down (or side to side) within the scroll bar. This allows you to move through more of the page at a time.

• **Click** inside the **vertical (or horizontal) scroll bar**. This moves the page up or down (or side to side) one screen at a time.

• **Click** on the **double arrows**. The double arrow will move chart a complete screen view in whatever direction arrow was selected.

Navigating the Fields

When you work in the main entry screens of Family Tree Maker, you will need to jump from field to field to enter the appropriate information. Since much of what is taking place at this time is done on the keyboard, keyboard commands are the easiest way to do this.

1. **Click** on the **Family Page button**. The Family Page window will appear.

2. Navigate through the **fields** using one of the following methods:

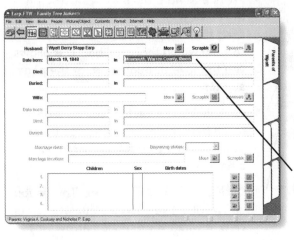

- **Press** the **Tab key** to move from one field to another within the Family Page.

- **Press** the **Enter key** to move from one field to another within the Family Page.

- **Press** the **up arrow or down arrow** to move from one field to another within the Family Page.

As you move through the fields, each field that the cursor arrives at will be highlighted.

NOTE

When you navigate in the Family Page using any of the keyboard commands, you will notice that you move from one field to the next where typing is allowed. Family Tree Maker will bypass any other options on the page.

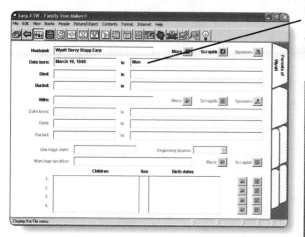

3. Type some new **information** in one of the fields. The highlighted field's information will change.

CAUTION

You do not want to use this method to change the order of children. Do not simply highlight the child in question and type the name of the new child. Doing this simply changes the name of the already entered individual; it does not rearrange the children. Methods of rearranging children are examined in Chapter 4, "Enhancing the Family."

Understanding the Different Views

Family Tree Maker offers different views to display the family data. Some of these views are limited to a single-family unit, while others display multigenerational charts of ancestors, descendants, or both.

Exploring the Family Page

The Family Page is where you will spend the most time. This is where you'll enter much of your data and where you'll access the other areas in which data can be entered.

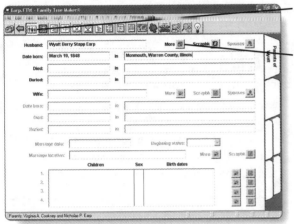

1. **Click** on the **Family Page button**. The Family Page will appear.

2. **Click** on the **More button**. The More About window will appear.

3. **Click** on the **Go Back button**. The Family Page will appear.

4. **Click** on the **Scrapbk button**. The Individual Scrapbook window will appear.

5. Click on **View**. The View menu will appear.

6. Click on **Family Page**. The Family Page will appear.

> ## NOTE
>
> If the individual in the Family Page has no spouse on that page, then the Spouses button will be disabled or "grayed out." The Spouses button is used when there is already a spouse in the Family Page for the individual in question.

7. Click on the **Spouses button**. The Spouses of dialog box will open.

> ## NOTE
>
> You will work more closely with the Spouses of dialog box in Chapter 3, "Family Tree Maker for Beginners."

Looking at the Individual Facts Card

The Individual Facts Card offers you everything you can access through the Family Page buttons in one easy-to-use window, complete with tabs and options.

1. **Click** on **View**. The View menu will appear.

2. **Click** on **Individual Fact Card**. The Individual Facts Card window will appear.

NOTE

When you are in the Family Page, the only way to access the Individual Facts Card is through the View menu.

NOTE

To learn how to work with the Individual Facts Card, see Chapter 9, "Getting into Individual Facts Cards."

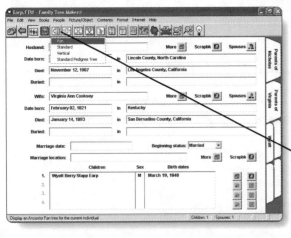

Working with the Ancestor Tree

The Ancestor Tree view offers a chart of the ancestors of a selected individual. There are four different formats in which to display this information.

1. **Click** on the **Ancestor Tree button**. The Ancestor Tree menu will appear.

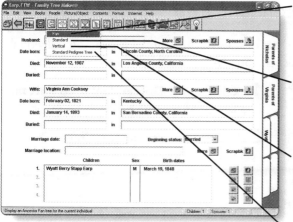

2a. **Click** on **Fan**. The Fan Chart will appear.

OR

2b. **Click** on **Standard**. The Standard Ancestor Tree will appear.

OR

2c. **Click** on **Vertical**. The Vertical Ancestor Tree will appear.

OR

2d. **Click** on **Standard Pedigree Tree**. The Standard Pedigree Tree will appear.

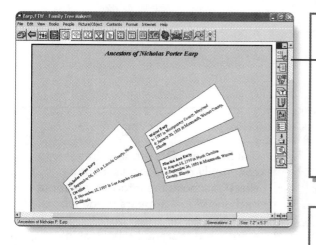

NOTE

Use the scroll bars to view the information about the individuals in the selected person's lineage. Additional information on ancestor trees is discussed in Chapter 13, "Looking at the Tree Reports in Family Tree Maker."

TIP

If the report is too small to read, you can use the Zoom In button found in the buttons along the right hand side of the chart to make the chart bigger.

Working with the Descendant Tree

The Descendant Tree view offers a chart of the descendants of a selected individual. There are two different formats in which you can display this information.

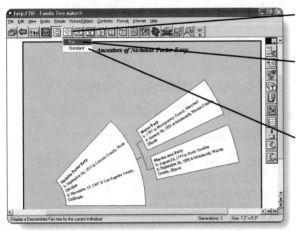

1. **Click** on the **Descendant Tree button**. The Descendant Tree menu will appear.

2a. **Click** on **Fan**. The Fan Chart will appear.

OR

2b. **Click** on **Standard**. The Standard Descendant Tree will appear.

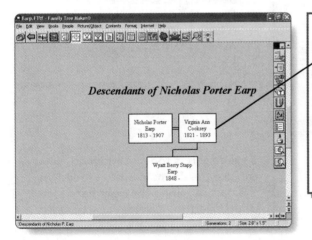

NOTE

The Standard Descendant Tree is commonly referred to as a "box chart" because the information about each individual appears inside a box. Double lines between boxes indicate a marriage or parental relationship. Single lines between boxes indicate a child or sibling relationship.

Working with the Hourglass Tree

The Hourglass Tree view offers a chart of both the descendants and ancestors of a selected individual. There are two different formats in which you can display this information.

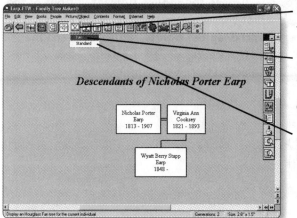

1. **Click** on the **Hourglass Tree button**. The Hourglass Tree menu will appear.

2a. **Click** on **Fan**. The Fan Chart will appear.

OR

2b. **Click** on **Standard**. The Standard Hourglass Tree will appear.

NOTE

The Standard Hourglass Tree also uses the box format to display ancestors and descendants.

Moving Information

Family Tree Maker allows you to use Windows' Copy and Paste functions to move information from field to field.

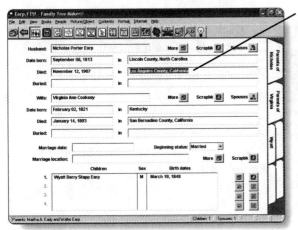

1. **Place** the **mouse pointer** in front of the first character you want to select and **click and drag** the **pointer** until you reach the last character you wish to cut or copy. The selected text will be highlighted.

2. **Click** on **Edit**. The Edit menu will appear.

3. **Click** on either **Cut Text or Copy Text**. The selected text will be placed on the Clipboard.

NOTE

The Cut Text command removes the text from the highlighted field and places it on the Clipboard. The Copy Text command leaves the text in the highlighted field and creates a copy on the Clipboard.

4. **Click** in the **field** where you want to paste the information.

5. **Click** on **Edit**. The Edit menu will appear.

6. **Click** on **Paste Text**. The copied (or cut) text will appear in the field you selected.

Exiting Family Tree Maker

You now have seen the basics of the Family Tree Maker program. When you are finished working in the program, you will want to close it.

1. **Click** on **File**. The File menu will appear.

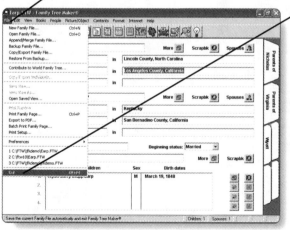

2. **Click** on **Exit**. Family Tree Maker will close.

TIP

You can also close the program by clicking the Close button ([X]) in the upper-right corner of the Family Tree Maker window.

3

Family Tree Maker for Beginners

Most of your time with Family Tree Maker will be spent entering the data you have uncovered about your family. At first, this information will be about yourself, your parents, and perhaps your grandparents. However, eventually you will find yourself with ancestral lines that go back many generations. Family Tree Maker helps you keep that information straight. In this chapter, you'll learn how to:

- Enter a primary individual
- Enter an event
- Change the date format
- Add a spouse
- Add children
- Add an additional spouse
- Move a child to the primary individual position

Entering a Primary Individual

Family Tree Maker allows you to record the information for each individual in your family history. The Family Page lets you enter specific information for the husband, wife, and children.

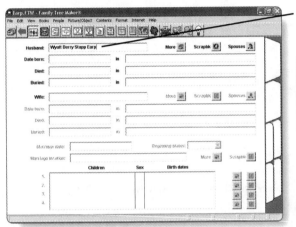

1. Type the **husband's name** in the Husband field.

NOTE

The primary individual can be entered in either the Husband field or the Wife field, depending on his or her gender.

TIP

An individual's name is made up of given names (first and middle names) and the surname (last name), typed in that order.

2. Press the **Tab key**. The cursor will move to the Date born field.

NOTE

Notice that when the Tab key is pressed, it bypasses the options to the right of the husband's name. These features are accessed by clicking on them or by pulling down the appropriate menu item.

Understanding Names in Family Tree Maker

Generally, when entering the name of an ancestor in Family Tree Maker, you will simply type the name (as it appears in the record or resource you are viewing) directly into the Name field in Family Tree Maker's Family Page. However, there are a few instances where the surname (last name) is not just a single word. In such instances, it is necessary to identify the surname for Family Tree Maker. This is done by surrounding the surname with backward slashes (\). There are many different reasons that a surname may be more than one word. This is especially true in the research of European names. Here are some examples, with the backward slash mark included, to give you an idea of what such a name should look like:

George \de la Vergne\

Peter \Van Der Voort\

Pierre \Bourbeau dit Lacourse\

Teresa \Garcia Ramirez\

Another instance in which you might need to use backward slashes is when entering someone who does not have a last name, such as a person of Native American descent. For instance, your ancestor might have been known as Running Bear. This name would be entered in Family Tree Maker as Running Bear\\.

Entering an Event

When you record your family history, you first must concentrate on names, dates, and places. Therefore, Family Tree Maker includes these basic fields in the Family Page.

1. Type a **date** in the Date born field.

NOTE

Family Tree Maker offers a date calculator for calculating dates when age and one date are known. See "Calculating Dates and Ages" in Chapter 20 "Working with Dates and Facts."

2. Press the **Tab key**. The cursor will move to the next field.

TIP

The traditional method for recording dates is to enter the numerals of the day, followed by the first three letters of the month, followed by the full four numerals of the year. Family Tree Maker defaults to a different setting. You'll learn how to change this setting later in this chapter, in the "Changing the Date Format" section.

---

3. If known, **type** a **birth location** in the **in field**.

4. Press the **Tab key**. The cursor will move to the Died field.

NOTE

When you enter the name of the place, use commas to separate the different divisions. Places should always be entered from smallest division, such as a town, to largest division, such as a state or country. Generally the country is omitted when it is the United States.

---

5. Type a **date** in the Died field, if known.

6. Press the **Tab key**. The cursor will move to the in field.

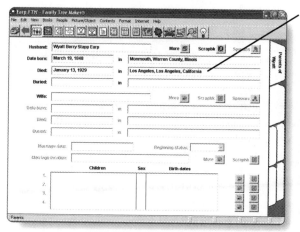

7. Type a **location** in the in field, if known.

Changing the Date Format

As mentioned earlier, Family Tree Maker's default for dates does not coincide with the standard followed in the genealogical community. However, this is easy enough to change.

1. Click on **File**. The File menu will appear.

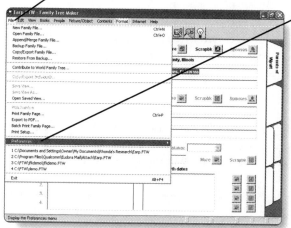

2. Move the **mouse** pointer to **Preferences**. The Preferences menu will appear.

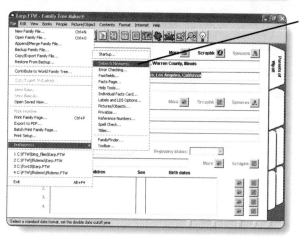

3. Click on **Dates & Measures**. The Dates & Measures dialog box will open.

NOTE

In the Dates & Measures dialog box, you can set the cutoff date for double dating. Double dating was the result of the change from the Julian to the Gregorian calendar. The Gregorian calendar determined that January would be the first month of the year. This took place for England, one of the last countries to change, and its colonies in 1752.

4. **Choose** the **DMY option** to conform to standard genealogical dating. The option will be selected.

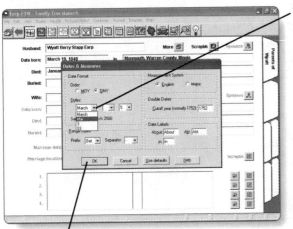

5. **Select** the **Month style** from the Styles drop-down list. The standard method is to use the first three letters of the month.

NOTE

The standard for dates in genealogy is the day followed by the first three letters of the month and then the four digit year.

TIP

Similar drop-down lists are available for changing the separator between the day, month, and year, and also for the format of the number of each day.

6. **Click** on **OK**. The Dates & Measures dialog box will close.

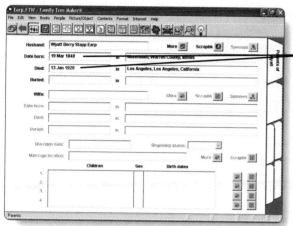

NOTE

The selections made in the Dates & Measures dialog box will automatically take effect in the Family Page.

Adding Individuals

Researching family history involves recording names, dates, and places. Programs like Family Tree Maker help make that easier by keeping track of the familial connections as you enter them.

Adding a Spouse

The Family Page is designed to include information about the husband, wife, and children, and it provides you with data fields in which you can type certain basic facts about each one. Now that you have entered the information about the husband, it is time to add the wife.

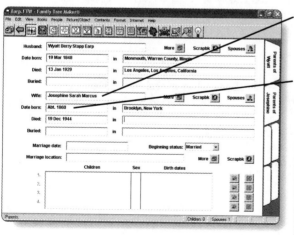

1. **Type** the **wife's name** in the Wife field and **press** the **Tab key**. The cursor will move to the Date born field.

2. **Enter** the **birth date** in the Date born field and **press** the **Tab key**. The cursor will move to the in field.

NOTE

If you do not know the exact date of an event, you can use the Abt. abbreviation to show that you are estimating that date. In other words the individual was born "about 1860."

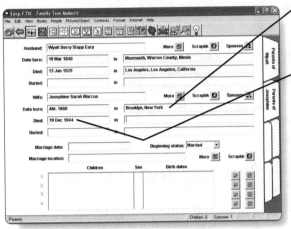

3. **Type** the **place of birth** in the in field and **press** the **Tab key**. The cursor will move to the Died field.

4. **Enter** the **death date** in the Died field and **press** the **Tab key**. The cursor will move to the in field.

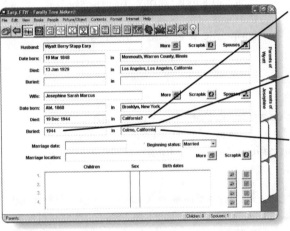

5. **Type** the **place of death** in the in field and **press** the **Tab key**. The cursor will move to the Buried field.

6. **Enter** the **burial date** in the Buried field and **press** the **Tab key**. The cursor will move to the in field.

7. **Type** the **place of burial** in the in field and **press** the **Tab key**. The cursor will move to the Marriage date field.

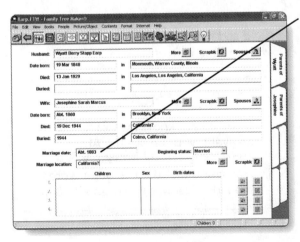

8. **Enter** the **marriage date** in the Marriage date field and **press** the **Tab key** twice. The cursor will move to the Marriage location field.

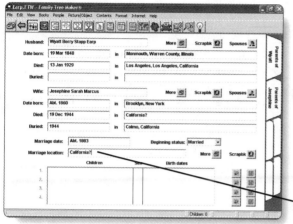

9. **Type** the **place of marriage** in the Marriage location field.

Adding Children

When you add children in the Family Page, you can enter the basics about each child. You can easily enter each child's full name, gender, and date of birth.

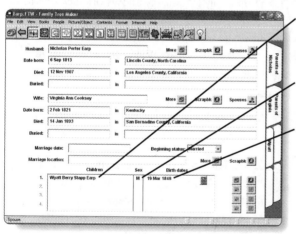

1. **Type** the **name** of the first child in the 1 field and **press** the **Tab key**. The cursor will move to the **Sex** field.

2. **Enter** the **sex** and **press** the **Tab key**. The cursor will move to the Birth dates field.

3. **Type** the **date of birth** and **press** the **Tab key**. The cursor will move to the 2 field for the name of the next child.

NOTE

You can add as many children as necessary. When you press the Tab key after each birth date, Family Tree Maker takes you to the next child line, where you can enter the information for the next child. For more on this, see Chapter 4, "Enhancing the Family."

Adding an Additional Spouse

The Family Page only allows one spouse to be displayed at a time. However, there are times when a researcher needs to enter more than one spouse for an individual. Family Tree Maker can support multiple spouses.

1. In the Family Page, **click** on the **Spouses button**. The Spouses of dialog box will open.

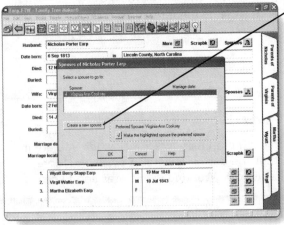

2. Click on the **Create a new spouse button**. A message box will appear, asking if you want the new spouse to be associated with the children previously entered for an individual.

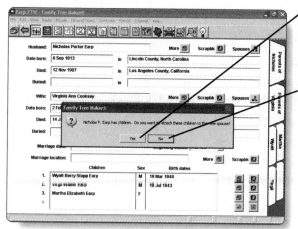

3a. **Click** on **Yes**. The children will have the new spouse as one of their parents.

OR

3b. **Click** on **No**. The children will not have the new spouse added as their parent.

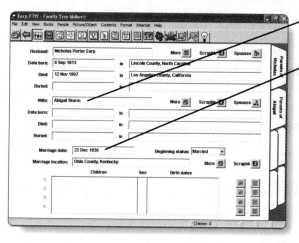

4. In the Wife field, **type** the **name** of the new spouse.

5. **Enter** the **information** you know about the marriage event.

Designating a Preferred Spouse

Family Tree Maker requires that one spouse be selected as the preferred spouse when you are working with reports and displaying the family in the Family Page window.

1. In the Family Page, **click** on the **Spouses button**. The Spouses of dialog box will open.

NOTE

Notice that the Spouses button now displays two individuals. This lets you know that the individual has more than one spouse.

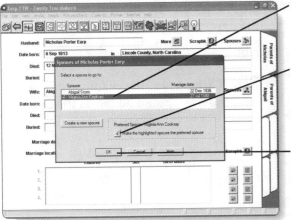

2. **Click** on the **spouse** you want as the preferred spouse. The spouse will be highlighted.

3. **Click** on the **Make the highlighted spouse the preferred spouse button.** The preferred spouse character will show at the left of the selected individual.

4. **Click** on **OK**. The Spouses of dialog box will close.

Switching to Another Spouse

Because you can only view the information and children of one spouse, it is necessary to switch spouses when you want to work on that specific family. You also need to change spouses if you want to add additional information about that particular marriage.

1. **Click** on the **Spouses button**. The Spouses of dialog box will open.

2. **Select** the **spouse** for the marriage on which you want to work. The spouse will be highlighted.

3. **Click** on **OK**. The Spouses of dialog box will close.

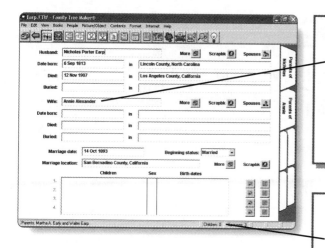

NOTE

The Family Page now displays the selected spouse. However, you have not made this spouse the preferred spouse. You can edit information about the spouse or the marriage or add additional children at this point.

TIP

Family Tree Maker will tell you how many children and spouses are known for the individual highlighted in the Family Page.

Moving a Child to the Primary Individual Position

After you have entered the children, it is possible that you will want to concentrate on a specific child. To do this, you move that child to the primary husband or wife position.

1. **Drag** the **scroll bar** next to the children information until you find the child with whom you want to work.

NOTE

The names that appear in the tabs at the right of the screen will change as the names in the Children section change.

2. **Click** on the **tab** for the selected child.

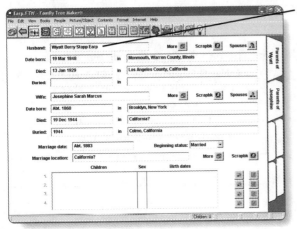

The child will replace the parent in the Husband or Wife field, and all of the other fields on the Family Page will change in accordance with the information currently known about that child.

Part I Review Questions

1. How do you open Family Tree Maker? *See "Starting Family Tree Maker" in Chapter 1*

2. How do you create a new Family File? *See "Creating a New Family File" in Chapter 1*

3. How do you discover the keyboard shortcuts available in Family Tree Maker? *See "Using Menus" in Chapter 2*

4. How are dialog boxes used in Family Tree Maker? See *"Understanding Dialog Boxes" in Chapter 2*

5. What are the three ways to move from one field to another in Family Tree Maker? *See "Navigating the Fields" in Chapter 2*

6. What are some of the main views found in Family Tree Maker? *See "Understanding the Different Views" in Chapter 2*

7. In what view do you enter the name of an ancestor? *See "Entering a Primary Individual" in Chapter 3*

8. How can you change the way dates are displayed in Family Tree Maker? *See "Changing the Date Format" in Chapter 3*

9. Can you have more than one spouse for an individual? *See "Adding an Additional Spouse" in Chapter 3*

10. How do you make the child the primary individual? *See "Moving a Child to the Primary Individual Position" in Chapter 3*

Using Family Tree Maker Features

4

Enhancing the Family

The family structure in a genealogical search is constantly changing. You are always finding new individuals that need to be connected in your database. In this chapter, you'll learn how to:

- Add parents
- Add siblings
- Line up children
- Add additional parental links

Adding Parents

It is likely that when you were working through Chapter 3, "Family Tree Maker for Beginners," you entered information about your immediate family. Now you want to add the parents of one of those people you entered.

1. Click on the **Family Page button**. The Family Page will appear.

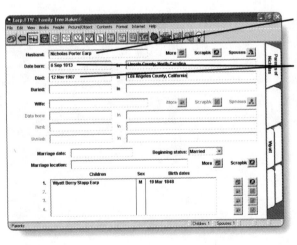

2. Click on the **Parents tab** for either the husband or the wife. The new Family Page window with the basic information for one child will be displayed. The child whose basic information is displayed is the individual who was the husband or wife in the previous screen.

3. Enter the **father's name** in the Husband field.

4. Enter the **father's birth and death information** in the appropriate fields.

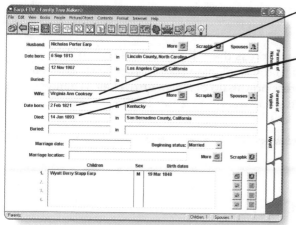

5. **Enter** the **mother's name** in the Wife field.

6. **Enter** the **mother's birth and death information** in the appropriate fields.

TIP

When typing the names of females, you will always enter them with their maiden name. That is the surname they had at birth.

NOTE

There will be times when you do not know the maiden name of the woman. The proper way to enter an unknown surname is to use the following set of characters: [--?--]. However, be aware that Family Tree Maker will question such a surname.

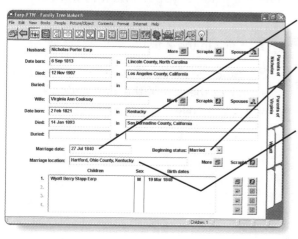

7. **Type** the **parents' marriage date** in the Marriage date field.

8. **Select** a **beginning status** from the Beginning status drop-down list. You will probably choose Married for this option.

9. **Enter** a **marriage location** in the Marriage location field.

TIP

If you prefer not to use your mouse, press the Tab key after entering the marriage date. This will take you to the Beginning status drop-down list. You can then change the status by pressing the up or down arrow key. When you have selected the Beginning status you want, press the Tab key to move the cursor to the Marriage location field.

Working with Children

When working in the Family Page, you will find that there are times when you need to add additional siblings. Additionally, it is through the Children fields that you have the opportunity to add another set of parents in addition to the child's natural, or biological, parents.

Adding Siblings

After you have added the information for the parents, you will want to work on your ancestor's siblings.

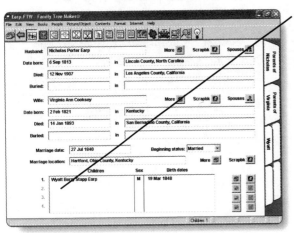

1. Click in the **2 field**.

2. Type the **name** of the next known child, as well as the rest of the information known about that child.

3. Enter the **next child's information** and continue to **add information** for the rest of the children in the family.

NOTE

There will be times when the children you have entered are not in their correct birth order. You will learn how to adjust their order in the "Arranging Child Order" section later in this chapter.

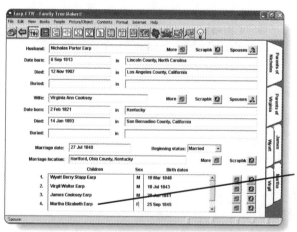

Adding Another Set of Parents

Due to adoption, there will be times when you will have two sets of parents for an individual. Or, in other cases, an individual might have a stepparent. Naturally, you want to record all the information for that person.

1. Click on the **child** you wish to select. The child will be selected.

2. Click on **People**. The People menu will appear.

3. Click on **Other Parents**. The Parents of dialog box will open.

NOTE

If the people you want to add as new parents have already been entered into the Family file, you will want to follow the steps in "Linking Children to Their Parents" found in Chapter 12 "Fixing Relationships & Duplicates."

4. Click on the **Create new parents button**. The Create New Parents dialog box will open.

5. Choose between **Two new parents**, **Another father**, or **Another mother**.

NOTE

Notice that when you select Another father or Another mother, the relationship options reflect the selection. You can only change the relationship for the chosen parent.

6. Click on the **down arrow** in the Relationship with field. The Relationship with drop-down list will appear.

7. Select the appropriate **relationship** from the list.

8. Click on **OK** to accept the selection. The Create New Parents dialog box will close and a message box will appear, asking you whether the child's siblings should be attached to the new parent(s).

9a. Click on **Yes** to attach the siblings to the new parent(s).

OR

9b. Click on **No** to attach only the selected child to the new parent(s).

10. Type the **parent's name** in the appropriate name field. Notice that the information for the remaining parent has carried over, and that the child's information has been brought to the new screen.

Arranging Child Order

In a perfect world, you would already know everything about all the children in a particular family. However, this is not usually the case. There will be times when you will need to add a child or change the order of the children previously entered.

Adding a Child

The best way to add an additional child to the list of children is to select the Insert Child option.

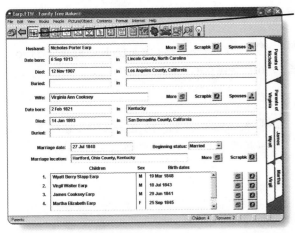

1. **Click** on the **Family Page button**. The Family Page window will open.

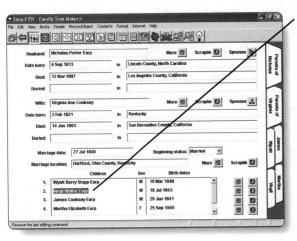

2. In the Children field, **click** on the **row** where you want to insert the new child.

3. **Click** on **People**. The People menu will appear.

4. **Click** on **Insert Child**. Family Tree Maker will insert a blank child row.

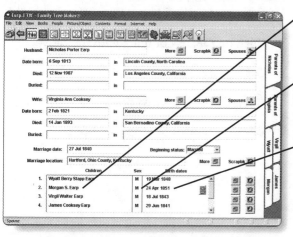

5. **Enter** the **name** of the new child and **press** the **Tab key**. The cursor will move to the Sex field.

6. **Type** the **sex** of the new child and **press** the **Tab key**. The cursor will move to the Birth dates field.

7. **Enter** the **birth date** of the new child.

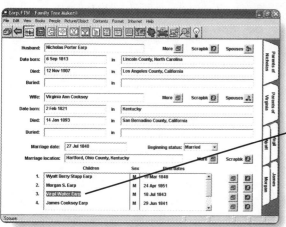

Moving a Child

After you have entered or updated a child's information, you might need to move the child so that he or she appears in the proper birth order.

1. **Select** the **child** you wish to move. The child will be selected.

2. Click on **People**. The People menu will appear.

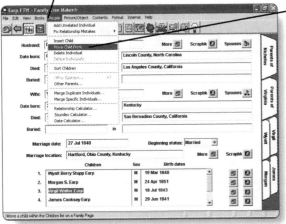

3. Click on **Move Child From**. A message box will appear, telling you how to move the child into a new position in the Children list.

4a. Enter the **birth date** of the new child.

Click on **OK** to continue with the move.

OR

4b. Enter the **birth date** of the new child.

Click on **Cancel** to stop the move.

5. In the Children field, **click** on the **position** where you want to move the child.

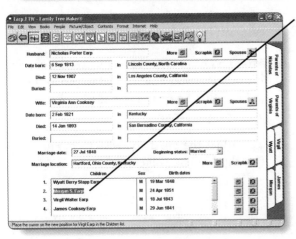

6. Click on **People**. The People menu will appear.

7. Click on **Move Child To**. The child will move to the new position.

CAUTION

To move a child, you cannot just type over the previously entered child's name. Family Tree Maker uses internal tracking that is not altered when you do this. If there are spouses or descendants associated with the original child, such a manual change could ruin the links previously created.

NOTE

Family Tree Maker will question any change where you type over the name of a previously entered individual, in order to find out if it should create a new individual.

TIP

If you discover that you have not moved the correct child or you want to undo what you have done, use the Undo command, found in the Edit menu.

Sorting Children

If you are working with records that do not list the children in order, it is not necessary to figure out the correct order before entering them on the Family Page. Family Tree Maker offers a Sort command that will rearrange the children chronologically after you have entered them.

1. Click on **People**. The People menu will appear.

2. Click on **Sort Children**. A dialog box will appear, confirming that you want to sort the children by birth order (oldest first).

3. Click on **OK** to have Family Tree Maker arrange the children in this order.

5

Documenting Sources

Citing the sources on which you are relying is one of the most important aspects of your research. Citing sources helps you keep track of the records you have used, which helps you avoid wasting time revisiting sources. In this chapter, you'll learn how to:

- Determine where you can cite a source
- Cite a source
- Create a master source
- Change a master source
- Search for a master source

Where Can You Cite Sources?

Family Tree Maker makes it possible for you to cite sources for the names of individuals and each of their specific events. This allows you to document your research so that others with whom you share information will know what you used to draw your conclusions.

1. **Click** on the **Family Page button**. The Family Page will appear.

2. **Click** on **View**. The View Menu will appear.

3. **Click** on **Source**. The Source-Citation dialog box will open.

You can cite sources in several fields, including these:

- Name

- Birth date and location

- Death date and location

- Burial date and location

- Marriage date and location

- Marriage ending date and location

- Each of the Fact fields

- Cause of death

- Medical information

Citing a Source

There are a few steps you need to take to create a source and cite it as proof of an individual event (or of a person's life as a whole). You will first create a master source listing; then, you can select it from a listing when you want to cite that source again.

Creating a Master Source

The master source is information about a source that doesn't change. For example, the author, title, and publication information don't change for a book. However, items like the page number from which the information comes will change depending on the person about whom you are entering data.

1. **Click** on **Edit**. The Edit menu will appear.

2. **Click** on **Edit Master Sources**. The Master Source dialog box will open.

TIP

You only need to enter a source one time. You can then recall it from the list the next time you want to cite it as proof of an individual's specific event. This is especially useful when a lot of information comes from a single source, such as a book. Remember that for every event or conclusion you include in your Family File, you should have a source cited.

3. **Type** the **book title** in the Title of source field and **press** the **Tab key**. The rest of the fields will be activated and the cursor will move to the Author/Originator field.

NOTE

The Title of source field has been programmed so that the title will print out in italics when source citations are included on reports.

4. **Enter** the **author's name** in the Author/Originator field and **press** the **Tab key**. The cursor will move to the Publication facts field.

5. **Type** the **publication information**.

TIP

Publication information includes the place of publication, the name of the publishing company, and the copyright date. The format is Anytown, Florida: Anywhere Publishing Company, 2002.

6. **Select** the **type of media** from the Source media drop-down menu.

NOTE

Including the source media type enables you to quickly see what the original source was. This will help you later, when you need to evaluate the proof used in drawing the conclusions you made.

7. **Type** the **call number** in the Call number field and **press** the **Tab key**. The cursor will move to the Source location field.

NOTE

The call number is the number assigned to the source in the repository where it was found. This could be a microfilm number, a Dewey Decimal system number, or some other numbering system unique to that particular library or archive.

8. **Enter** the **source location** and **press** the **Tab key**. The cursor will move to the Comments field.

NOTE

The source location might be a library, archive, county courthouse, or cousin's residence. The source location is where the original source exists. Recording this gives you a place to turn should you need to revisit the original.

9. **Type** your **comments** and **press** the **Tab key**. The cursor will move to the Source quality field.

NOTE

The Comments section offers you a place to put your thoughts about the source and the information included in that source. This information is not included when the source is printed on reports; it is only for your personal reference.

10. **Enter** the **quality** of the source.

NOTE

The quality of the source is a reference to how reliable the source is. If the source is difficult to read because of unclear handwriting or faded ink, it is possible that the information found could be inaccurate.

11. **Click** on **OK**. The Master Source dialog box will close.

Using the Source-Citation Dialog Box

The Source-Citation dialog box is where you will select the appropriate master source for the information you are citing. You can enter source information when you enter the data and details for each ancestor.

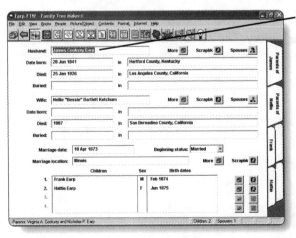

1. **Click** in the **field** where you want to add a source citation.

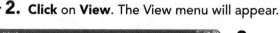

2. Click on **View**. The View menu will appear.

3. Click on **Source**. The Source-Citation dialog box will open.

TIP

You can also use the keyboard shortcut Ctrl+S to launch the Source-Citation dialog box. Whether you access it this way or through the menu, the source citation will be attached to the highlighted field or the last field in which you were working.

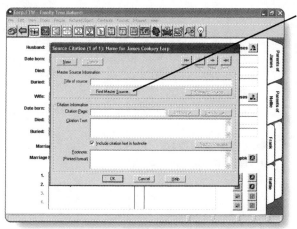

4. Click on the **Find Master Source button**. The Find Master Source dialog box will open.

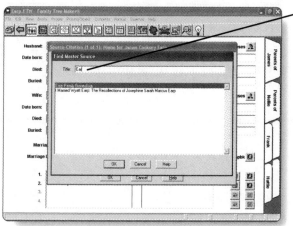

5. Type part of the **title** in the Title field. Family Tree Maker will highlight the first title that matches the word you've typed.

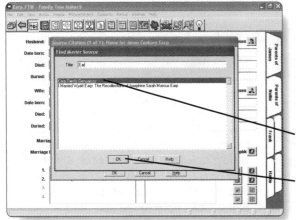

TIP

If you have a lengthy list of sources, you can use the scroll bar to quickly scroll through the list.

6. **Click** on the desired **source** in the list. The source will be selected.

7. **Click** on **OK**. The Find Master Source dialog box will close.

NOTE

Notice that the title of the source and the printed format of the footnote are now displayed in the Source-Citation dialog box.

8. **Type** the **page number** of the citation in the Citation Page field.

NOTE

Not all source citations will have a page number included on this screen. For more information about source citations, read Elizabeth Shown Mills's *Evidence! Citation and Analysis for the Family Historian* (Genealogical Publishing Co., 1997).

9. Enter the **Citation text** in the Citation Text field. The citation text might be further identifying information. For instance, when citing a census record, you would want to include the Enumeration District, Supervisor's District, Dwelling number, and Family number for the specific house of your ancestor on that census page.

TIP

You can decide whether to include text from the Citation Text field in the printed footnote. Click on the Include citation text in footnote check box if you want the text to be included. If the text is just for your information, make sure the box is not checked.

10. Click on **OK** to close the Source-Citation dialog box.

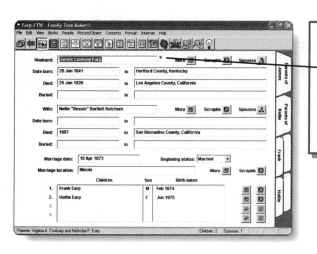

NOTE

Notice that there is now an "s" next to the field where you elected to cite the source. This is how you know that you have cited a source for either an individual or an event.

Creating a Master Source from the Source-Citation Dialog Box

Few of us are so organized that we already know all of the sources that we will be citing before we begin. While you're working on a family, you might find that an obscure source was not added to the master source list earlier. You do not need to exit out of the Source-Citation dialog box to add a master source.

1. **Press Ctrl+S** to open the Source-Citation dialog box.

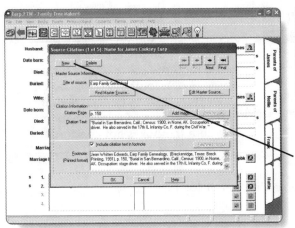

NOTE

It is possible that the Source-Citation dialog box already has a previously cited source. You can have more than one source citation per person or event.

2. **Click** on the **New button**. Family Tree Maker will start a new source citation, and the cursor will move to the Title of source field.

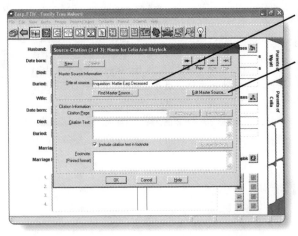

3. **Type** the **title** of the new source. The Edit Master Source button will be activated.

4. **Click** on the **Edit Master Source button**. The Master Source dialog box will open.

TIP

Notice that the Title of source field has been disabled in the Master Source dialog box. You cannot change the title at this time. For more information on editing master sources, see the "Changing a Master Source" section later in this chapter.

5. **Enter** the **appropriate source information**.

6. **Click** on **OK**. The Master Source dialog box will close.

You can now complete the source citation with the page number and citation text as you learned in the "Using the Source-Citation Dialog Box" section earlier in this chapter.

7. **Click** on **OK**. The Source-Citation dialog box will close.

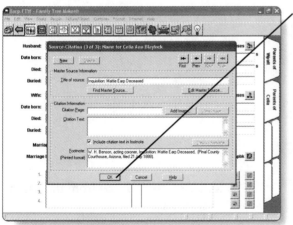

Changing a Master Source

While we would all like to think we are perfect, there will be times when an error is discovered. In a source, that should be fixed as soon as it is noticed. Usually you will notice such an error when you're working with that source in the Source-Citation dialog box.

1. Click on **View**. The View menu will appear.

2. Click on **Source**. The Source-Citation dialog box will open.

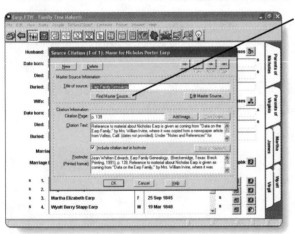

3. Click on the **Find Master Source button**. The Find Master Source dialog box will open.

4. Select a **master source** from the list of available sources.

5. Click on **OK**. The Find Master Source dialog box will close. You will notice that the Edit Master Source button has now been activated in the Source-Citation dialog box.

6. **Click** on the **Edit Master Source button**. The Master Source dialog box will open.

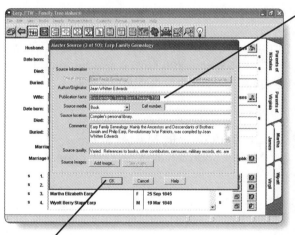

7. **Make** the appropriate **changes** to the master source fields. Usually you'll be changing a typo or fixing the publication date.

NOTE

The Title of source field is grayed out when you access the master source in this manner. To edit the title of a master source, see "Editing a Master Source" in the next section.

8. **Click** on **OK**. The Master Source dialog box will close.

Editing a Master Source

While accessing the master source through the Source-Citation dialog box is easy, you cannot change the title of the source this way. If you have a lot of editing to do to a master source, you might want to go directly to the master source.

1. Click on **Edit**. The Edit menu will appear.

2. Click on **Edit Master Sources**. The Master Source dialog box will open.

TIP

You can use the First, Prev, Next, and Final buttons to skip through previously entered master sources. Click on the New button to create a new master source, and use the Delete button to delete the currently displayed master source.

NOTE

If you inadvertently type over the name of a source in the Source-Citation dialog box, Family Tree Maker will ask you whether you want to change the present title or create a new source.

Searching for a Master Source

There will be times when you will want to look at a specific master source. The easiest way to do this is through the Master Source dialog box.

1. Click on **Edit**. The Edit menu will appear.

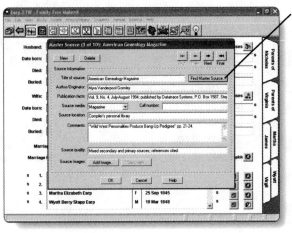

2. Click on **Edit Master Sources**. The Master Source dialog box will open.

3. Click on the **Find Master Source button**. The Find Master Source dialog box will open.

NOTE

You then would type in the first few letters of the source in question as you did earlier in this chapter when working in "Using the Source-Citation Dialog Box."

TIP

You can also use the scroll bar along the right side of the list to scroll through the list of master sources.

Attaching Images to Sources

Modern technology affords us the opportunity to scan documents or microfilm to digitize documents. Family Tree Maker offers you the ability to attach such an image to the Master Source or the specific Source-Citation dialog box.

1. Press Ctrl + S. The Source-Citation dialog box will open.

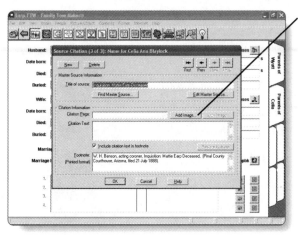

2. Click on the **Add Image button**. The Get Image From dialog box will open.

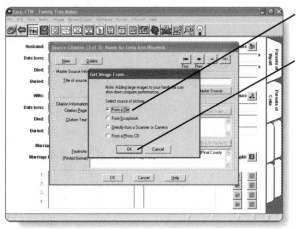

3. Select the appropriate **source** of the picture. The option will be selected.

4. Click on **OK**. Family Tree Maker will open a window or launch the appropriate program.

NOTE

For more on working with images in Family Tree Maker, see Chapter 17, "Creating a Scrapbook."

6

Understanding More About Options

Family history is much more than just names and dates of birth or death. As you research further into your family's generations, you will be keeping track of additional events and wanting to add family stories. In this chapter, you'll learn how to:

- Add and work with additional facts
- Add addresses for living relatives
- Track medical information
- Work with the More About Lineage window

Working with the More About Facts Window

Family Tree Maker offers you a way to track additional life events. As your research progresses, you will find that you are relying on such things as probate records and church records, in addition to the more recognizable vital records. Family Tree Maker has included a variety of predefined facts (Family Tree Maker's name for the events in a person's life) to help you record this information.

1. **Click** on the **Family Page button**. The Family Page will appear.

2. **Click** on the **More button**. The More About window will appear.

3. **Click** on the **Facts button**. The More About Facts window will appear.

NOTE

You can also access the More About options from the View menu.

Adding Additional Facts

You will record much of the information about your ancestors in the More About Facts window. This is where you will record the variety of life events that you discover.

1. Click on the **Fact down arrow**. The Fact drop-down menu will appear.

2. Click on a **fact** in the menu. The fact will be selected and the menu will close.

3. Press the **Tab key** to advance to the Date field.

TIP

Many of the facts in the Fact drop-down menu are pertinent to specific religions. This allows you to select the appropriate religious event, rather than making do with, say, a general christening event.

4. Type the **date** of the event and **press** the **Tab key**. The cursor will move to the Comment/Location field.

TIP

Information entered using the More About options can also be added using the Individual Facts Card. For more on this option, see Chapter 9, "Getting into Individual Facts Cards."

5. **Enter** the **comment/location** for the fact and **press** the **Tab key**. The new fact will be added, in chronological order, to the list of facts for that individual, for those events with full dates.

NOTE

The Pref'd check box is disabled for event-type facts, unless you have conflicting or duplicated facts. If you had two death dates, you would select one of them as your preferred choice.

Adding Additional Names

There are times when you will discover that your ancestor had another name. It might have been a religious name or a nickname, or it might just be a variant of his or her given name. Family Tree Maker allows you to keep track of these different names. Whereas the AKA (also known as) name option allows you to record one additional name, through the name options here you can record variant name spellings and other names you simply want to remember.

1. **Click** on the **Fact down arrow**. The Fact drop-down menu will appear.

2. **Select** the **Name fact** and **press** the **Tab key**. The cursor will move to the Comment/Location field.

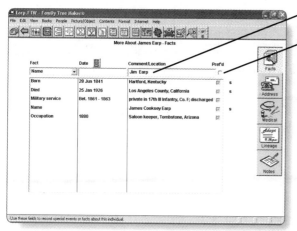

3. **Enter** the **individual's name**.

4a. **Click** on the **Pref'd check box** if you want this name to be the one used in the Family Page and on reports.

OR

4b. **Leave** the **Pref'd check box** empty if you do not want this name used in the Family Page and on reports.

Selecting a Preferred Name

Even if you checked the Pref'd check box when you entered a name, you can always change that. For example, when sending reports to a cousin, you might want to use one name; when sharing with your brother or sister, you might want to use another name.

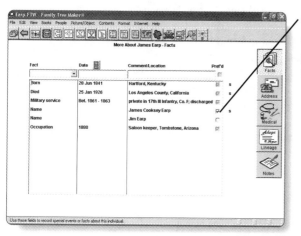

1. **Click** in the **Pref'd check box** next to the name you want to select. The selected name will have a check mark in the check box.

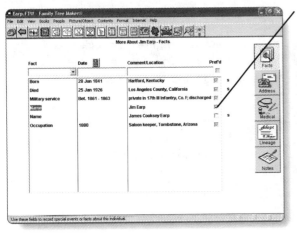

2. **Click** in the **Pref'd check box** next to another name fact. Notice that, in addition to displaying the check mark, the preferred name will appear at the top of the list of name facts.

Creating a New Fact Name

Family Tree Maker includes 41 different facts, but you might need to record an event that is not covered by any of them. You can create a new fact name whenever you need one.

1. **Click** in the **Fact field**.

2. **Type** the **name** of the new event and **press** the **Tab key**. The cursor will move to the Date field.

3. **Enter** the **date** and **press** the **Tab key**. The cursor will move to the Comment/ Location field.

NOTE

You can use partial dates, or estimate the date based on the individual's age at another time. To estimate dates, see "Calculating Dates and Ages" in Chapter 20, "Working with Dates and Facts."

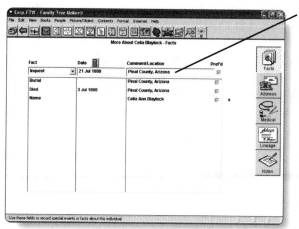

4. **Type** the **event location** and **press** the **Tab key**. Family Tree Maker will open a New Fact Name message box, verifying that you want to accept the new fact name.

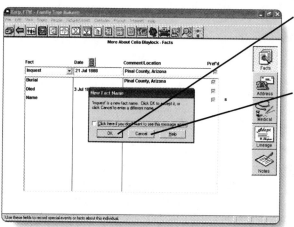

5a. **Click** on **OK** to accept the new fact name. The new fact name will be saved.

OR

5b. **Click** on **Cancel** to return to the Fact field to type in a different name or select a different predefined fact.

NOTE

You can always get rid of a fact name that you have created. For more information on this, see Chapter 20, "Working with Dates and Facts."

Using the Address Window

The Address window is useful when you're entering data about your living relatives. People involved with a family association rely heavily on this for mailing lists, as do those who want to keep track of cousins with whom they are exchanging information.

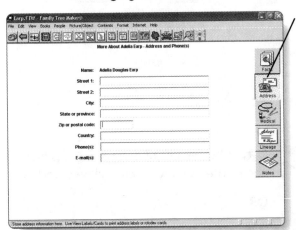

1. **Click** on the **Address button**. The More About Address and Phone(s) window will appear.

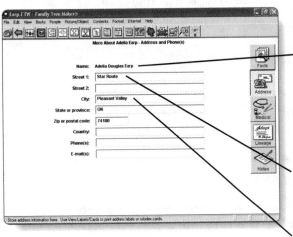

NOTE

Notice that the individual's name has already been supplied. Family Tree Maker assumes you are entering the address for the individual currently in the More About window.

2. **Type** the **street address** in the Street 1 field and **press** the **Tab key** twice. The cursor will move to the City field.

3. **Type** the **city name** and **press** the **Tab key**. The cursor will move to the State or province field.

4. Type the **state or province** and **press** the **Tab key**. The cursor will move to the Zip or postal code field.

5. Enter the **zip or postal code** and **press** the **Tab key**. The cursor will move to the Country field.

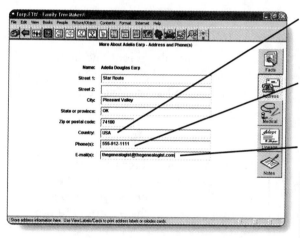

6. Type the **country name** and **press** the **Tab key**. The cursor will move to the Phone(s) field.

7. Enter the **phone number** and **press** the **Tab key**. The cursor will move to the Email(s) field.

8. Enter the **e-mail address**.

TIP

Just because there are fields for all this information does not mean you need to supply it. You need only put in what is important for you to be able to contact the individual at a later date.

Working with Medical Information

Modern medical technology has made understanding your medical family tree more important than ever before. Family Tree Maker provides you with space for recording pertinent medical information about your family members and ancestors.

1. **Click** on the **Medical button**. The More About Medical window will appear.

2. **Type** the **height** in feet and inches in the Height field and **press** the **Tab key**. The cursor will move to the Weight field..

TIP

To move between feet and inches, or pounds and ounces, you can either press the Tab key or use your mouse pointer to click in the appropriate box.

3. **Enter** the **weight** in pounds and ounces in the Weight field and **press** the **Tab key**. The cursor will move to the Cause of death field.

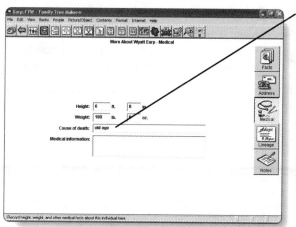

4. Type the **cause of death** and **press** the **Tab key**. The cursor will move to the Medical information field.

NOTE

The cause of death will generally be the medical term found on the death certificate, or the illness or condition that caused the individual to die.

5. In the Medical information field, **enter** the **details** you feel are important about your ancestor's medical history.

NOTE

The Medical information field can hold up to 200 characters of information, which is about five lines of text.

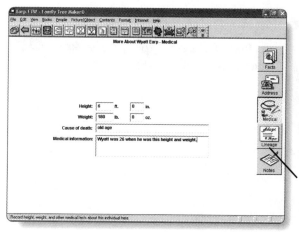

Opening the More About Lineage Window

Family Tree Maker uses the More About Lineage window to organize information about relationships, titles, and aliases.

1. **Click** on the **Lineage button**. The More About Lineage window will appear.

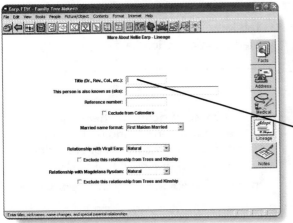

2. **Enter** any appropriate **information** or **select** one of the available **relationship options**. The next sections will describe how to use these fields and relationship options.

TIP

When entering a title, do not enter items such as Jr. or III. The titles entered here will be printed in front of the individual's name on reports. If your ancestor was a Jr. or a Sr., this is typed into the Name field on the Family Page, at the end of the name and following a comma. When you are indexing your book, the comma becomes necessary in order to distinguish Jr. from the surname. Roman numerals such as III or IV are automatically recognized by Family Tree Maker, so no comma is necessary.

Entering AKA Names

There will be times when you will discover a name change or an alternate name for your ancestor or family member. Legal name changes are just one way the AKA field can be used.

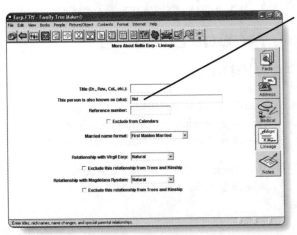

1. **Click** in the **This person is also known as (aka) field** and **type** the **also known as name** for your ancestor.

TIP

When you print reports, you can elect to use the also known as name instead of or in addition to the name used in the Family Page. Such decisions are made when you are working in the report. For more on this topic, see Chapter 16, "Creating Genealogy Style and Genealogical Source Reports."

Working with Special Relationships

As you dig deeper into your family history, you are apt to discover mothers who died early, fathers who remarried, adoptions, and other unique relationship situations. It is natural to want to record these in Family Tree Maker.

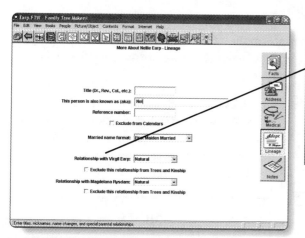

NOTE

You will want to pay attention to the names in the Relationship section. How these individuals will be connected to each other will be affected as you make changes in the Relationship section.

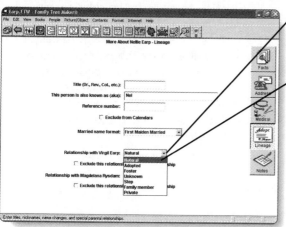

1. **Click** on the **Relationship with down arrow** next to the father's name. The Relationship drop-down menu will appear.

2. **Select** the appropriate **relationship** between the father and the individual.

NOTE

You will only be able to select Natural from the drop-down menu for one father and one mother, regardless of how many parents you have added to a person.

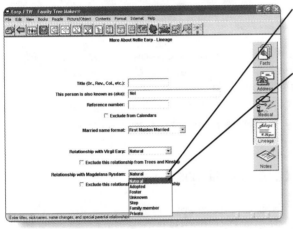

3. **Click** on the **Relationship with down arrow** next to the mother's name. The Relationship drop-down menu will appear.

4. **Select** the appropriate **relationship** between the mother and the individual.

Excluding Relationships

At times you might want to exclude information from reports you send to family members, possibly out of respect for their feelings. Some of those exclusions are set up in the More About Lineage window.

1. **Click** on the **Exclude this relationship from Trees and Kinship check box** for either the mother or the father of the individual. The option will be selected and that relationship will be excluded from your reports.

NOTE

Electing to exclude the relationship from Trees and Kinship will affect reports. Kinship reports and Ancestor Trees will exclude the paternal and/or maternal ancestors, depending on which relationship(s) you chose to exclude. Descendant trees will exclude the child and the child's descendants.

7

Using More About Notes

One way to make your family history interesting to other family members is to include family stories. With Family Tree Maker you can do just that. In this chapter, you'll learn how to:

- Enter notes and stories
- Copy and move notes and stories
- Find text in notes
- Import notes
- Export notes
- Format notes for printing

Working with Notes and Stories

Most of us have heard our grandparents, aunts, or uncles share stories about family members. As your research progresses, you will find additional stories. Family Tree Maker's More About Notes section allows you to incorporate these notes and stories into your research.

Entering Notes and Stories

The More About Notes window allows you to enter, in a narrative style, the stories or research notes you want to include in your reports. Be sure you have the individual you want to enter notes about selected in the Family Page.

1. **Click** on **View**. The View menu will appear.

2. **Move** the **mouse pointer** to More About. The More About menu will appear.

3. **Click** on **Notes**. The More About Notes window will appear.

TIP

Remember you can always use the More About button beside the individual you have selected to open the More About window, where you will find the More About Notes button.

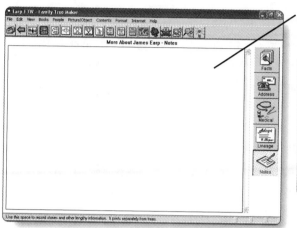

4. In the text box, **enter** the **text** you wish to include for the individual.

> ## NOTE
>
> The information typed into the Notes window will not print on the family tree styled reports. However, you can print this information on a family group sheet report or include it in a book.

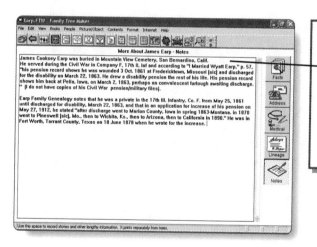

> ## TIP
>
> When quoting information from a source, be sure to include the source citation information. Always put quotation marks around any information that is a direct quote from a published source.

Copying Notes and Stories

Sometimes a particular note might apply to more than one individual. When you are working with such a story, you will want to take advantage of the copy and paste functions available in Family Tree Maker.

1. Click on **View**. The View menu will appear.

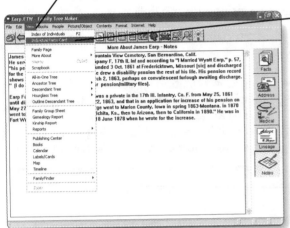

2. Click on **Individual Facts Card**. The Individual Facts Card will appear.

3. Click on **Notes**. The Notes tab will appear.

TIP

This is another method of getting to the Notes window for a particular individual.

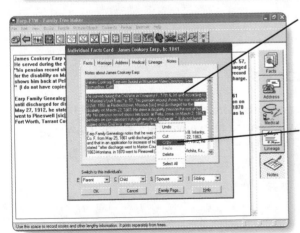

4. Click and drag the **mouse pointer** to highlight the desired text. The text will be selected.

5. Right-click on the selected **text**. The right mouse menu will appear.

6. Click on **Copy**. The selected text will be placed on the Clipboard, ready for you to paste wherever you like. Chapter 10, "Searching Your Family Tree File," explains how to locate someone in your database who is not included in the current Family

Page window. You can use these functions to locate an individual to whose Notes window you want to paste the copied text.

TIP

The menu that appears when you right-click is a shortcut menu that allows you to cut, copy, paste, or delete selected text. This is the same as clicking on the Edit menu and selecting the options there.

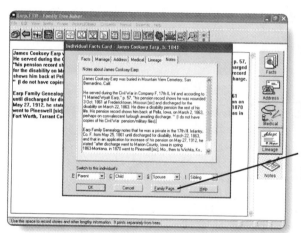

Moving Notes and Stories

You might discover that a story you thought pertained to one individual was really about another. The easiest way to fix this is to move the story from one More About Notes window to another.

1. Click on the **Family Page button**. The Family Page window will appear.

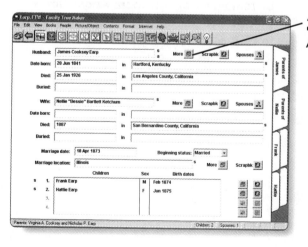

2. Click on the **More button**. The More About window will appear.

NOTE

If you were last working in a More About Notes window, then the More About Notes window will be displayed when you click the More button for another person. If you weren't working in a More About Notes window earlier, then you will need to click on the Notes button.

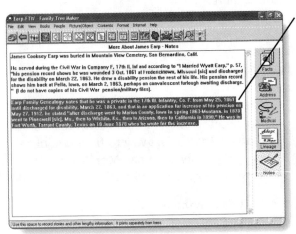

3. **Click and drag** the **mouse pointer** to highlight the selected text.

4. **Click** on **Edit**. The Edit menu will appear.

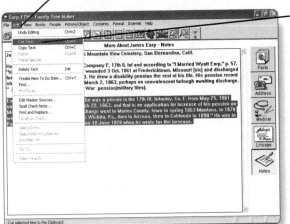

5. **Click** on **Cut Text**. The selected text will be removed from the More About Notes window and placed on the Clipboard, ready to be pasted in another individual's More About Notes window.

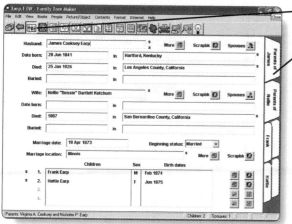

6. **Click** on the **Family Page button**. The Family Page window will appear.

7. **Click** on the **Name tab** of the individual you want to select. The Family Page window will change to reflect the selected individual.

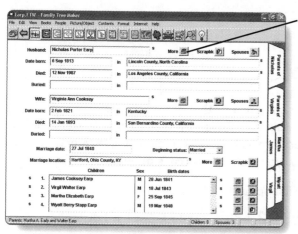

8. **Click** on the **More button**. The More About window will open. The More About Notes window should be displayed because it was the last More About window used.

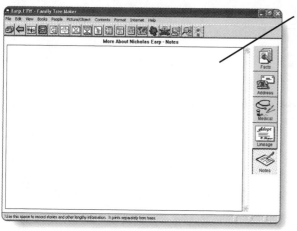

9. **Click** inside the **text box**.

10. **Click** on **Edit**. The Edit menu will appear.

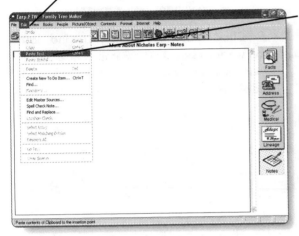

11. **Click** on **Paste Text**. The text will appear in the More About Notes window.

TIP

The keyboard shortcuts Ctrl+X for Cut, Ctrl+C for Copy, and Ctrl+V for Paste can be used instead of the menus.

Finding Text in Notes

It can be hard to find one particular sentence or thought when you have typed a large amount of text in the More About Notes window. Family Tree Maker offers a way to search for a specific word or phrase. Before you follow these directions, be sure the More About Notes window you want to search is open.

1. **Click** on **Edit**. The Edit menu will appear.

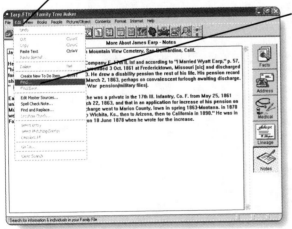

2. **Click** on **Find**. The Find dialog box will open.

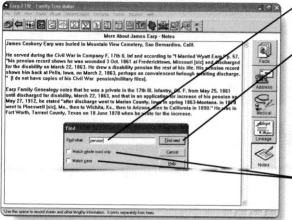

3. **Type** the **word or phrase** for which you want to search in the Find what field.

4. **Click** on the **Find next button**. When Family Tree Maker finds the requested word or phrase, it will highlight it in the More About Notes window.

TIP

Family Tree Maker allows you to match whole words or match case. This allows you to eliminate those words that share consecutive letters with the word for which you are looking. Selecting the match case option will look only for words that have letters capitalized or lower case as you have them entered in the Find what field.

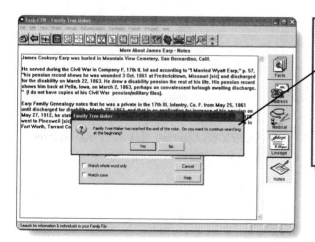

NOTE

If the cursor was not at the beginning of the text in the More About Notes window, then Family Tree Maker might ask you if you want to continue searching from the beginning. Click on Yes if you want to continue searching.

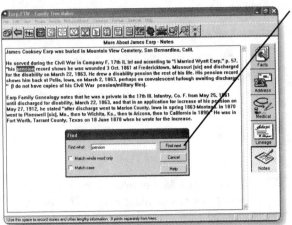

5. Click on the **Find next button** to continue searching the text.

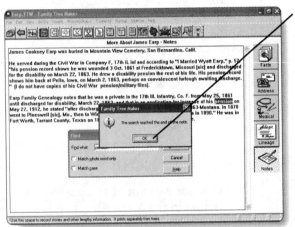

6. Click on **OK** when you see the message box telling you that Family Tree Maker has reached the end of the text. The message box will close and you will be returned to the Find dialog box.

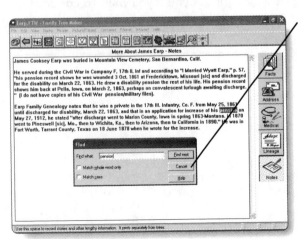

7. Click on **Cancel**. The Find dialog box will close.

Importing Text to Notes

At some point, you might want to import some text into Family Tree Maker. You might have received a write-up via e-mail, or you might have already typed up a family story that you now want to place in the More About Notes window. You can do so by importing the text or by copying and pasting.

Copying Text

The Windows operating system allows you to copy text from one application and paste it into another. Because Family Tree Maker is a Windows program, this option is available to you.

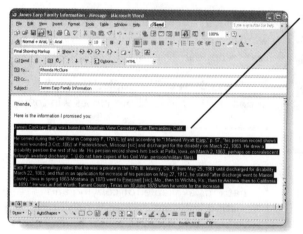

1. Highlight the **text** you want to copy from the e-mail message or word-processing file.

TIP

Note that you can use this same approach for copying information found online. Remember when copying from another's Web site to ask permission before taking any stories or narrative write-ups found.

---

2. Press Ctrl+C to copy the text. The text will be placed on the Clipboard.

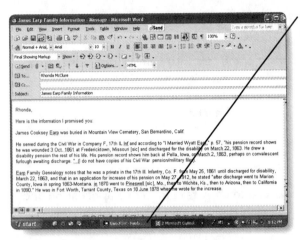

3. **Click** on **Family Tree Maker** in the Windows Taskbar. Family Tree Maker will be maximized.

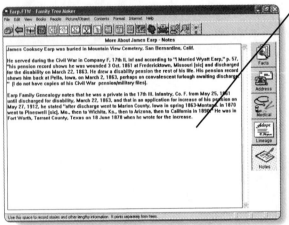

4. **Click** in the **More About Notes window,** at the location where you want the text to appear. The cursor will appear.

5. **Press Ctrl+V.** The copied text will appear in the More About Notes window.

NOTE

You have now used all the different methods available for copying and pasting information into Family Tree Maker. Some people prefer to use menu options while others like the keyboard commands. You will eventually settle on what works best for you.

Importing Text

Family Tree Maker also allows you to import text. This can be done only when the file you want to import ends in a .txt extension, because that is the only file type that Family Tree Maker recognizes. You need to have the cursor in the More About Notes window where you want the text to appear before you follow these steps.

1. Click on **File**. The File menu will appear.

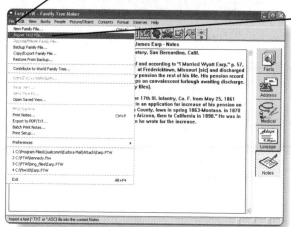

2. Click on **Import Text File**. The Import Text File dialog box will open.

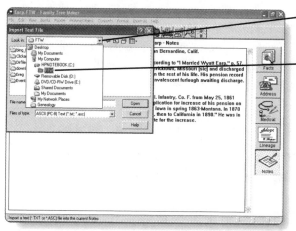

3. Click on the **Look in down arrow**. The Look in drop-down menu will appear.

4. Navigate to the **folder** where the text file is located.

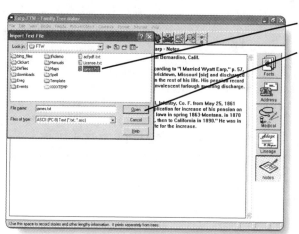

5. Click on the **selected file**.

6. Click on **Open**. The text will be placed in the More About Notes window.

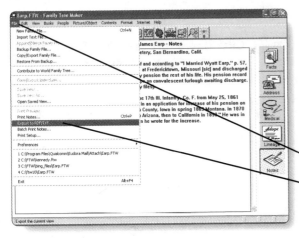

Exporting Notes

You might have notes that you have received from others, and in turn, you might want to share your notes with a relative or fellow researcher. You can do so by exporting the notes.

1. **Click** on **File**. The File menu will appear.

2. **Click** on **Export to PDF/TXT**. The Export dialog box will open.

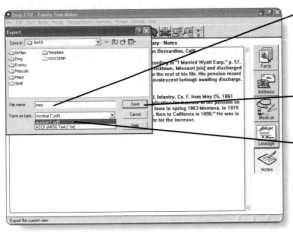

3. In the File name field, **type** the **name** of the file you want to export. You will want to pay attention to where the file is being saved so you can retrieve it later.

4. **Click** on the **Save as type down arrow**. The Save as type menu will appear.

5. **Select** between **PDF** and **TXT** formats. The Save as type file type will be selected.

NOTE

Family Tree Maker automatically defaults to the PDF file format, a portable document format that retains all style, graphics, and printer options. This file format is particularly useful when sharing charts and reports and posting to the Internet. You will learn more about this file format feature in "Saving the Tree in PDF Format" in Chapter 15, "Viewing and Printing Reports and Trees."

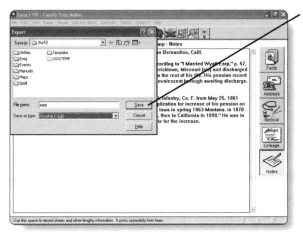

6. **Click** on **Save**. The text in the More About Notes window will be saved to the file.

Formatting Notes for Printing

With the More About Notes window open, you can format the text's chosen font, style, and size to alter how it appears when printed in the reports. This will make the notes stand out in your report.

1. **Click** on **Format**. The Format menu will appear.

2. **Click** on **Text Font, Style, & Size**. A message box will appear, reminding you that the changes made will display only when you print the report, not on the screen.

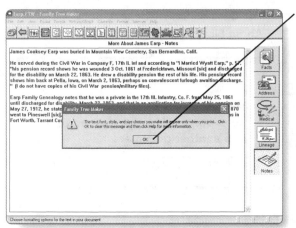

3. Click on **OK**. The message box will close and the Text Font, Style, & Size dialog box will open.

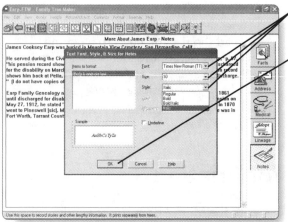

4. Select the desired **font**, **size**, and **style** from the drop-down menus.

5. Click on **OK**. The Text Font, Style, & Size dialog box will close.

NOTE

The formatting options, which are also used in the reports, are discussed in more detail in Chapter 15, "Viewing and Printing Reports and Trees."

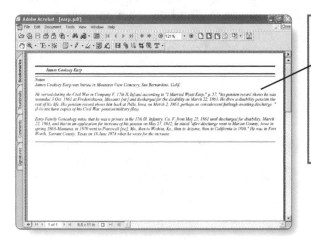

TIP

Formatting in the More About Notes window affects all the text in the Notes window, as seen here in this PDF export. You cannot highlight a single paragraph and change the style on just that single paragraph.

8

Working with More About Marriage

Much of what you have learned up to this point dealt with a specific individual in your database. However, the marriage event is unique, and Family Tree Maker understands that there are different ways to handle it. In this chapter, you'll learn how to:

- Add information on beginning marriage status
- Select an ending status for the marriage
- Work with reference numbers
- Select the appropriate marriage fact
- Select a preferred date
- Work with the Marriage Notes window

Accessing the More About Marriage Window

The More About Marriage window allows you to include notes or pertinent additional dates about the marriage of two individuals. While the marriage date itself can be entered on the Family Page, the additional notes and details are entered on the More About Marriage window.

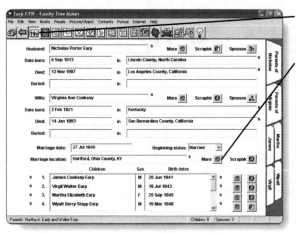

1. **Click** on the **Family Page button**. The Family Page window will appear.

2. **Click** on the **Marriage More button**. The More About Marriage window will appear.

3. **Click** on the **Facts button**. The More About Marriage Facts window will appear.

Using the More About Marriage Facts Window

The More About Marriage Facts window is where you can include additional details about a marriage. This is where you would include a divorce fact or a conflicting marriage fact.

1. Click on the **Ending status down arrow**. The Ending status drop-down menu will appear.

2. **Select** the appropriate **Ending status** from the menu.

NOTE

If you don't know how the marriage ended, you can select Unknown from the drop-down menu.

Entering a Reference Number

The Reference number field allows you to enter any numbers or letters you choose. If you have a unique filing or pedigree system, you might use this field for that system's reference number.

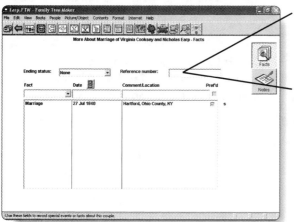

1a. **Type** a **reference number** in the Reference number field.

OR

1b. **Leave** this **field blank** if you do not have a reference numbering system.

NOTE

The Reference number field can hold up to 11 lowercase letters or numbers or combination thereof. The reference number can be any identification number that you would like to use. Some family associations use it for membership numbers.

Adding a Marriage Fact

Although you have already entered one marriage fact, there are others that you might need to enter—possibly a conflicting marriage date or a fact that details the end of that marriage.

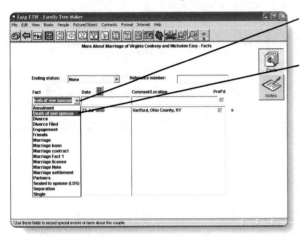

1. Click on the **Fact down arrow**. The Fact drop-down menu will appear.

2. Click on the **appropriate fact** from the menu and **press** the **Tab key**. The fact will be selected and the cursor will move to the Date field.

TIP

If you select something like the annulment, divorce, or death of one spouse, be sure to change the Ending status to correspond with the fact.

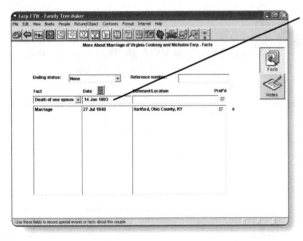

3. Enter the **date** of the fact in the Date field and **press** the **Tab key**. The cursor will move to the Comment/Location field.

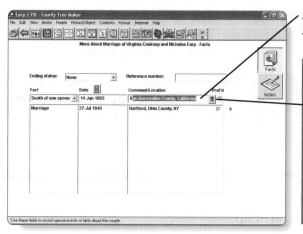

4. Type the **comment** or **location** of the fact.

TIP

The small trashcan that shows up when you type a previously-entered place allows you to "trash" what Family Tree Maker is suggesting. If the place is the one you want, you can press the Tab key to accept it and add the fact to the Facts list.

NOTE

There is a connection between the facts in the More About Marriage page and the marriage fact itself. To learn more about this and how it might pertain to unique situations in your research, see Chapter 20, "Working with Dates and Facts."

Using the Pref'd Check Box

The Pref'd (Preferred) check box is activated when you have selected a duplicate fact. This happens when you have two conflicting dates recorded.

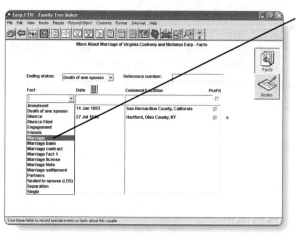

1. Select a **duplicate fact** from the Fact drop-down menu.

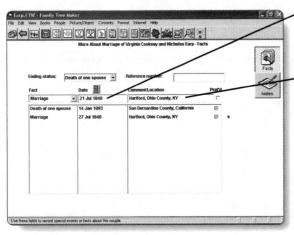

2. **Type** the **date** of the event in the Date field and **press** the **Tab key**. The cursor will move to the Comment/Location field.

3. **Type** the **comment** or **location** of the fact and **press** the **Tab key** twice. The new fact will appear in the Fact list.

NOTE

Notice that at this point the Pref'd check box is automatically selected. The newly added fact does not become the preferred fact. This means it will not be the marriage fact that appears in any reports that you print.

4. **Click** on the **Pref'd check box** for the second duplicated fact. The newly selected preferred fact will move to the top of the duplicated events and will have a check in the Pref'd check box.

Working with Marriage Notes

Just as you might include stories about an individual as a note, you might also want to record something about a marriage. As it does for individuals, Family Tree Maker supplies you with a More About Notes window for marriages.

1. **Click** on the **Notes button**. The More About Marriage Notes window will appear.

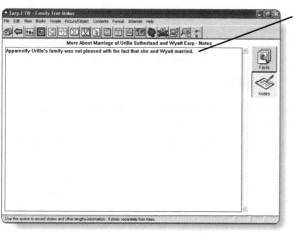

2. **Type** the **text** you want to include about the marriage.

3. Click on **Format**. The Format menu will appear.

4. Click on **Text Font, Style, & Size**. The Text Font, Style, & Size dialog box will open, so you can format your newly added note.

NOTE

Family Tree Maker will remind you that the changes you make to font, style, and size will appear only in your printed reports. Also, remember that these changes will affect the entire note, not just a section of it. Click on OK to close the message box.

NOTE

See Chapter 7, "Using More About Notes," to refresh your memory about changing the text in the More About Notes window.

9

Getting into Individual Facts Cards

With the More About button on the Family Page, you have the ability to enter a lot of different information about a person. Sometimes you want easy access to that information. The Individual Facts Card gives you instant access. In this chapter, you'll learn how to:

- Access the Individual Facts Card
- Establish the Individual Facts Card as a default for editing information
- Add a fact
- Add a note
- Switch to another related individual within the Individual Facts Card
- Add a new related individual to the Family File
- Go to the Family Page

Accessing the Individual Facts Card

The Individual Facts Card was designed to offer you instant access to the information and facts for an individual. You can access this card either through a menu option or through one of the reports.

Opening an Individual Facts Card

Regardless of the view you are using in Family Tree Maker, you can always get to the Individual Facts Card for the primary individual by using the menu option.

1. **Click** on **View**. The View menu will appear.

2. **Click** on **Individual Facts Card**. The Individual Facts Card window will appear.

NOTE

If you are in the Family Page, the View menu is the only way to open the Individual Facts Card.

Accessing the Individual Facts Card from Another View

While you are working in one of the Report or Tree views, you might notice that a fact isn't right or that you have a typo in a note. Using the Individual Facts Card, you can immediately correct the problem and then return to the Report or Tree view.

1. **Click** on a **report button**. The chosen Report or Tree view will appear.

NOTE

It may be necessary to select the type of report or tree from a drop-down menu after you have clicked on the Report or Tree button.

---

2. **Double-click** on the desired **individual**. The Individual Facts Card for that person will open.

Individual Facts Card Versus the Family Page

Family Tree Maker allows you to choose between the Individual Facts Card or the Family Page when working in other views. In other words, when you double-click on a person in a Report view, you can either be taken to that person's Individual Facts Card or to the Family Page for that person.

Determining Your Preference

You must first decide which you would prefer to open when working in other views.

1. **Click** on a **report button**. The chosen Report or Tree view will appear.

2. **Double-click** on the desired **individual**. The Individual Facts Card for that person will open.

When you have the Individual Facts Card selected as your default, you can make any changes to the individual and then click on OK to return to the Report or Tree view.

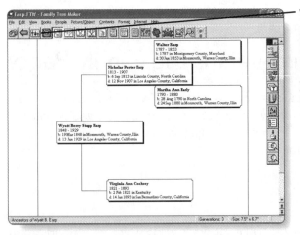

When you access the Family Page from a Report view, it is similar to clicking on the Family Page button in the toolbar. The Family Page replaces the Report view, and you can work in the More About window or Family Page from there.

TIP

If you are in the Family Page, you can return to the Report view by clicking on the Go Back button.

Establishing Your Preference in Family Tree Maker

Once you have experimented with accessing both the Individual Facts Card and the Family Page from any Report view, you will want to tell Family Tree Maker which you prefer as your default choice when double-clicking on an individual.

1. Click on **File**. The File menu will appear.

2. Move the **mouse pointer** to **Preferences**. The Preferences menu will appear.

3. Click on **Individual Facts Card**. The Individual Facts Card preferences dialog box will open.

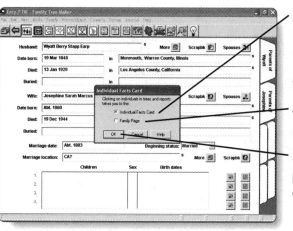

4a. Click on **Individual Facts Card**. The Individual Facts Card option will be selected.

OR

4b. Click on **Family Page**. The Family Page option will be selected.

5. Click on **OK**. The Individual Facts Card preferences dialog box will close and the default will be set.

Working with the Individual Facts Card

The Individual Facts Card dialog box offers you instant access to everything currently known about a given individual. You also have the ability to change or add information, and to select or add another related individual.

Adding a Fact

Through the Individual Facts Card, you have the ability to add just as many facts as you do using the More About window.

1. Click on **View**. The View menu will appear.

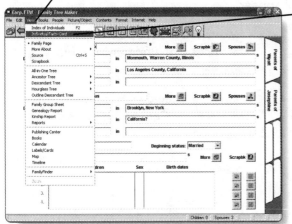

2. Click on **Individual Facts Card**. The Individual Facts Card dialog box will open.

NOTE

If you do not see the Fact, Date, and Comment Location fields above the list of facts for the given individual, you might need to change the display settings in Windows. When Large Fonts has been selected in the display settings, it sometimes forces the list of facts to sit on top of these three fields, which makes it look like they do not work or exist.

---

3. Click on the **Fact down arrow**. The Fact drop-down menu will appear.

4. Click on the **appropriate fact**. The fact will be selected and the list will disappear.

5. Press the **Tab key**. The cursor will move to the Date field.

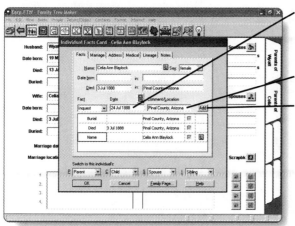

6. **Type** the **date** and **press** the **Tab key**. The cursor will move to the Comment/ Location field.

7. **Type** the **comment** or **location**.

8. **Click** on the **Add button**. The new fact will be added to the individual's list of facts.

TIP

Just like in the More About Facts window (see Chapter 6, "Understanding More About Options"), you can create new facts in the Individual Facts Card. Simply type the name of the new fact and press the Tab key. You can then follow steps 6 through 8 above.

Adding a Note

The tabs of the Individual Facts Card mirror the options found in the More About window, accessed from the Family Page. As such, anything that you can add in the More About windows can be added in the Individual Facts Card.

1. **Click** on the **Notes tab**. The tab will move to the front.

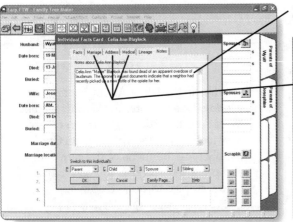

2. **Type** the **note**.

NOTE

You can access any of the other options, such as the Marriage, Address, or Medical sections, by clicking on the appropriate tab. This brings that section of the Individual Facts Card to the front so that you can work with it. All of these sections mirror their More About equivalents.

Switching to Another Related Individual

While the main menu items are disabled when the Individual Facts Card is open, you still can move to other related individuals. You can change the focus of the Individual Facts card by using the drop-down menus at the bottom of the card.

1. **Click** on one of the **down arrow choices**. The list of appropriate individuals will appear.

2. **Click** on the desired **individual**.

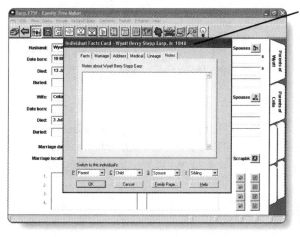

The individual will be selected and the Individual Facts Card will pertain to the newly selected individual.

Adding a New Related Individual

Often as you are entering information about an ancestor, you will find that the record or book that has supplied you with that information will also supply you with the name or details of a previously unknown, related individual. You can add this person using the Individual Facts Card.

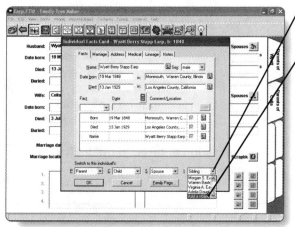

1. **Click** on the appropriate **down arrow**. The corresponding list will appear.

2. **Click** on the **Add a... menu option**. The menu will disappear and the Individual Facts Card will be blank.

3. **Type** in the **details** for the new person.

Closing the Individual Facts Card

When you are finished making changes or additions to the individual, you can close the Individual Facts Card. Depending on your choice, you will either be returned to the Report view or taken to the Family Page.

1a. **Click** on **OK**. The Individual Facts Card will close and you will be returned to the report view if you opened the Individual Facts card from the report.

OR

1b. **Click** on the **Family Page button**. The Individual Facts Card will close and you will be taken to the Family Page for that individual.

NOTE

If you select another individual or add a new individual and then click on OK, Family Tree Maker might ask you if you want to pull up a new tree with that individual included. You can click on Yes to redesign the tree/report, or you can click on No to revert back to your original tree/report. The information entered in the Individual Facts Card will not be lost if you choose No.

Part II Review Questions

1. How can you change the order in which children are listed? *See "Arranging Child Order" in Chapter 4*

2. Where can you cite a source in Family Tree Maker? *See "Where Can You Cite Sources" in Chapter 5*

3. How can you attach an image to a source citation? *See "Attaching Images to Sources" in Chapter 5*

4. How can you include additional life events for an individual? *See "Adding Additional Facts" in Chapter 6*

5. How can you copy and paste text in the Notes window? *See "Moving Notes and Stories" in Chapter 7*

6. Can you alter the form and style of notes for printing on reports? *See "Formatting Notes for Printing" in Chapter 7*

7. How do you access the More About Marriage window? *See "Accessing the More About Marriage Window" in Chapter 8*

8. Can you include more than just the marriage event in the More About Marriage facts? *See "Using the More About Marriage Facts Window" in Chapter 8*

9. What are the two ways to open an Individual Facts Card? *See "Accessing the Individual Facts Card" in Chapter 9*

10. Is it possible to add a new related individual to the Family File through the Individual Facts Card? *See "Adding a New Related Individual" in Chapter 9.*

PART III

Working in Family Tree Maker

10

Searching Your Family Tree File

When you first begin entering data, it is easy to use the tabs along the right side of the window to select the individual you want. However, after you have been researching for a while, you will discover that you have too many people in your files to do this effectively. In this chapter, you'll learn how to:

- Locate individuals using Quick Search
- Work with the Find feature
- Rearrange the index
- Search by name
- Search by other types of criteria
- Work in the FamilyFinder Center

Using Quick Search by Name

The Index of Individuals has a built-in quick search where you can easily type in the name of the individual for whom you are searching. This is the easiest way to locate an individual in your Family Tree file.

1. Click on **View**. The View menu will appear.

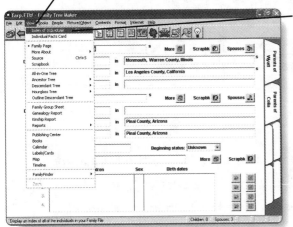

2. Click on **Index of Individuals**. The Index of Individuals dialog box will open.

> ## TIP
>
> There are two other ways to access the Index of Individuals dialog box. You can press the F2 key or click on the Index of Individuals button.

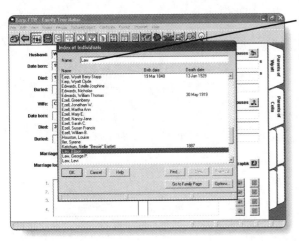

3. Click in the **Name field** and **type** the **surname** (last name) of the person you want to find. Family Tree Maker will move the highlight bar to different possible matches as you type.

NOTE

Notice that the highlight bar locates and moves to the first name that fits the letters you have entered. It is usually not necessary to type in the complete surname.

TIP

The Quick Search is not case sensitive. You can type the name in uppercase, lowercase, or mixed case.

Working with the Find Feature

There is a Find feature built into the Index of Individuals dialog box. This is an alternative for those times when the Quick Search is not available.

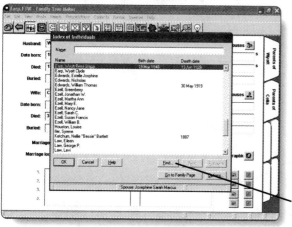

TIP

To find out more about when Quick Search is not available, see the "Rearranging the Index" section later in this chapter.

1. **Press** the **F2 key**. The Index of Individuals dialog box will open.

2. **Click** on the **Find button**. The Find Name dialog box will open.

3. In the Name field, **type** the **name** of the individual you want to find.

4. **Click** on **OK**. The Find Name dialog box will close and Family Tree Maker will highlight the first individual who fits your search.

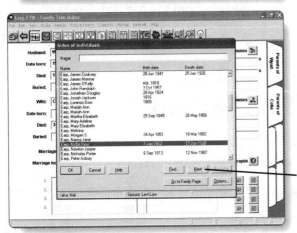

TIP

You do not need to type the entire name. You can type just the surname or the first name, and Family Tree Maker will go to the first individual with that name.

5. **Click** on **Next**. Family Tree Maker will highlight the next individual who fits your search.

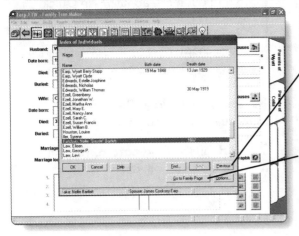

TIP

You can also click on the Previous button, and Family Tree Maker will highlight the previous individual who fit your search.

6. **Click** on the **Go to Family Page button**. The Index of Individuals dialog box will close and Family Tree Maker will display the Family Page for that individual.

TIP

If you are trying to return to a tree/report or some other window, you will want to click on the OK button, which returns you to the window you were working in before you opened the Index of Individuals dialog box.

Rearranging the Index

The default arrangement of the Index of Individuals is alphabetical by last name in ascending order. However, you might want to view the list in a different format.

1. Click on **View**. The View menu will appear.

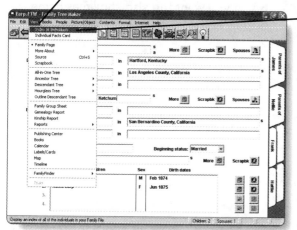

2. Click on **Index of Individuals**. The Index of Individuals dialog box will open.

3. Click on the **Options button**. The Options dialog box will open.

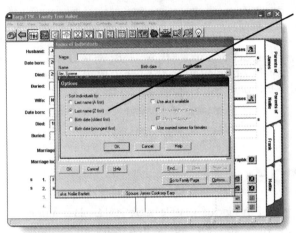

4. **Select** a different **radio button** in the Sort individuals by list. This will change the order of the Index of Individuals.

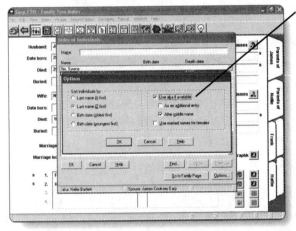

5. **Click** on the **Use aka if available check box** if you want the also known as name to display in the Index of Individuals.

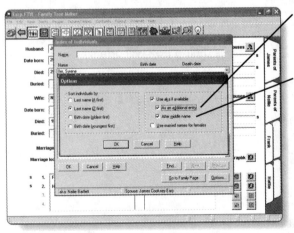

6. **Click** on the **As an additional entry check box**. Family Tree Maker will create a new entry in the Index using the nickname.

7. **Click** on the **After middle name check box**. Family Tree Maker will add the nickname to the original Index entry, placing it after the individual's middle name.

8. **Click** on the **Use married names for females check box**. Family Tree Maker will change the surname for each female in the index to display her married surname.

NOTE

Selecting the married names changes the surnames of all the females in the list so that they are listed by their married names instead of their maiden names, but it offers an easy way to list females for whom you don't have a maiden name.

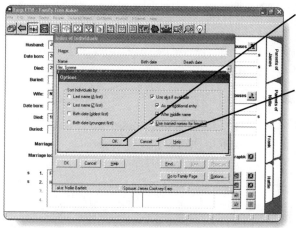

9a. **Click** on **OK**. The Options dialog box will close and your changes will take effect.

OR

9b. **Click** on **Cancel**. The Options dialog box will close, but the changes will not take effect.

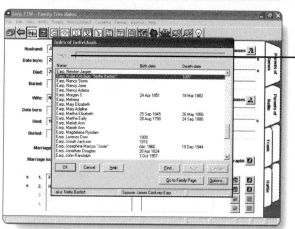

NOTE

If you have changed the Sort individuals by option to something other than Last name (A first), the Quick Search Name field will be disabled.

Using the Find Individual Feature

While you will often search for an individual by name or by scrolling through the Index of Individuals, Family Tree Maker understands that you might also need to look for individuals based on the year of an event or the place where events happened. You can do this using the Find Individual feature.

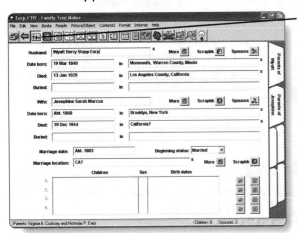

1. **Click** on the **Family Page button**. The Family Page window will appear.

> ### NOTE
>
> The Find Individual menu option is available only when you are in the Family Page.

2. **Click** on **Edit**. The Edit menu will appear.

3. **Click** on **Find Individual**. The Find Individual dialog box will open.

Searching by Name

Of course, you can still use the Find Individual feature to search for individuals by name, perhaps looking for everyone who shares a similar given or middle name.

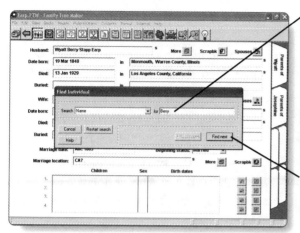

1. Type the **name** for which you want to search in the for field.

NOTE

The Find Individual dialog box defaults to a name search.

2. Click on the **Find next button**. Family Tree Maker will locate the first individual in the database with the name for which you are searching.

3. Click on the **Find next button** again. Family Tree Maker will display the next individual in the database with the name for which you are searching.

TIP

If you accidentally pass the individual you wanted, click on the Find previous button to go back in the search.

NOTE

You can re-create the same search by clicking on the Restart search button.

Searching by Date

At some point, you might want to determine who in your database was born or married on or prior to a specific date. The Find Individual feature has the ability to search for dates.

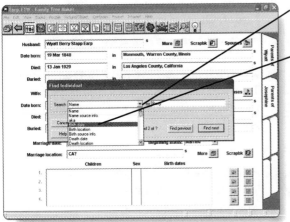

1. **Click** on the **Search down arrow**. The Search drop-down menu will appear.

2. **Click** on the **Birth date option** and **press** the **Tab key**. The option will be selected and the cursor will move to the for field.

NOTE

The example used describes searching for events on a specific date. There are many ways to enter dates in the the for field. For a complete list, see the table in Chapter 22 "Working with the Custom Report."

TIP

To select other Search fields, use the scroll bar in the Search drop-down menu.

3. **Type** the **date** in the for field.

4. **Click** on the **Find next button**. Family Tree Maker will display the first Family Page window with a date that fits the search criteria.

TIP

Continue to click on the Find next button until you find the individual in whom you are interested.

5. **Click** on **Cancel**. The Find Individual dialog box will close.

Searching by Location

After names and dates, the item in which researchers are most interested is location. The Find Individual feature allows you to search for a specific location.

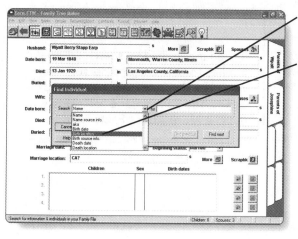

1. **Click** on the **Search down arrow**. The Search drop-down menu will appear.

2. **Click** on the **Birth location option** and **press** the **Tab key**. The option will be selected and the cursor will move to the for field.

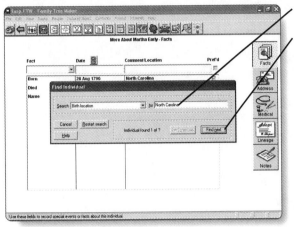

3. **Type** the **location** in the for field.

4. **Click** on the **Find next button**. Family Tree Maker will display the More About Facts screen for the first individual who fits the search criteria.

5. **Continue to click** on the **Find next button** until you find the individual in whom you are interested.

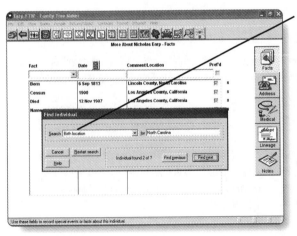

6. **Click** on **Cancel**. The Find Individual dialog box will close, and the More About Facts window for the last individual found will be displayed.

TIP

If the Find Individual search criteria applies to only a single person then when the Find Individual dialog box closes, the Family Page will display, not the More About Facts window.

Searching by Source

You can also use the Find Individual feature to search for a specific source or to determine for which events and individuals you have cited a source.

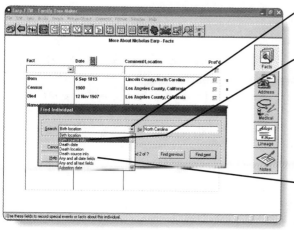

1. **Click** on the **Search down arrow**. The Search drop-down menu will appear.

2. **Click** on the **Birth source info option** and **press** the **Tab key**. The option will be selected and the cursor will move to the for field.

TIP

Selecting Any and all text fields is a quick way to look through all text fields for a word.

3. **Type** the **word** for which you are looking in the for field.

4. **Click** on the **Find next button**. Family Tree Maker will display the first individual's record that contains the word for which you are searching.

NOTE

To see the text in question, you must open the More About window and look through the text fields.

Searching by Comment

You might be interested in discovering for which individuals you have entered medical information or other comments. You can do this using the Find Individual feature.

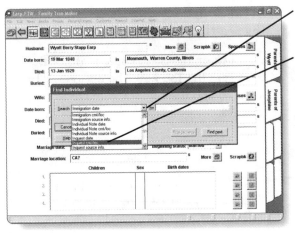

1. **Click** on the **Search down arrow**. The Search drop-down menu will appear.

2. **Click** on one of the **comment fields** in the menu and **press** the **Tab key**. The comment field you choose will appear in the Search field and the cursor will move to the for field.

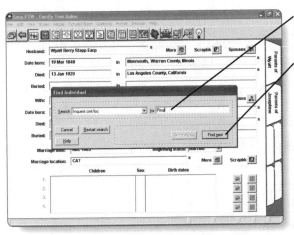

3. **Enter** the **word** for which you want to search.

4. **Click** on the **Find next button**. Family Tree Maker will display the More About screen for the first person who fits the search criteria.

TIP

To find comments with any text, replace the word with !=, and Family Tree Maker will show you everyone who has any text in that comment field.

Working with the FamilyFinder Center

The FamilyFinder Center offers a number of different methods for searching and researching. At this point, we will concentrate on how to use the FamilyFinder Search and view the generated report.

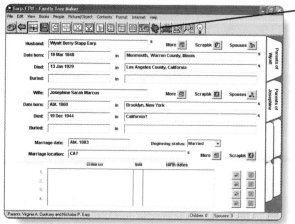

1. **Click** on the **FamilyFinder Center button**. The FamilyFinder Center will open.

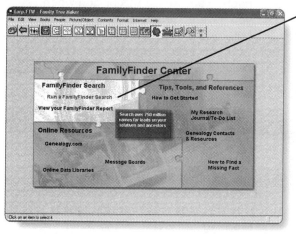

2. **Click** on **Run a FamilyFinder Search**. A message box will appear, asking you whether you want to create a FamilyFinder Report.

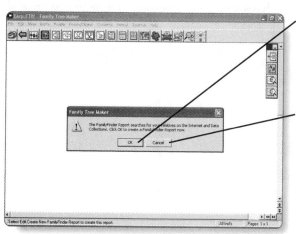

3a. **Click** on **OK**. The message box will close and the Create New FamilyFinder Report dialog box will open.

OR

3b. **Click** on **Cancel**. A blank FamilyFinder Report will be displayed.

4. **Select** either **All individuals** or **Selected individuals** in the Include section.

5. **Click** on **OK**. If you are connected to the Internet, your browser will launch. When the search is complete, a message box will appear, telling you how many matches were found.

NOTE

If you click on the Individuals to Include button, the Individuals to Include dialog box will open. You might want to use this option when you have added some new individuals but you do not want the report to be rerun for everyone in the family file.

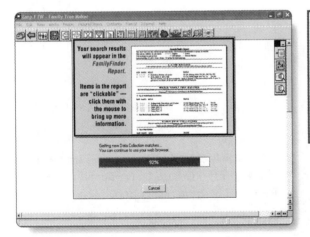

NOTE

See Chapter 14, "Working with Specialty Reports and the Research Journal," for more information on working with some of the other FamilyFinder Center options.

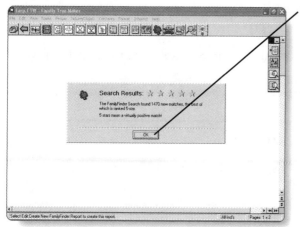

6. Click on **OK**. The FamilyFinder Report will be displayed.

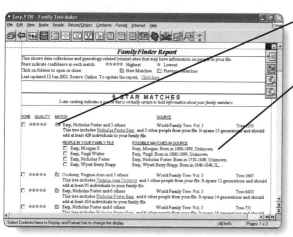

7. Click on the **file folder** for one of your matches. The FamilyFinder Report will give you more details about the match.

8. Click on the **possible match in source** and your browser will open and you will be taken to the appropriate online source.

NOTE

Some of the sources will require a subscription fee to access them.

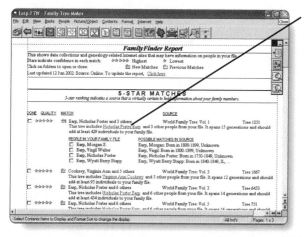

9. Double-click on the **ancestor's name**. The Individual Facts Card for that individual will appear.

TIP

The more stars next to an entry, the higher the probability of the match being your ancestor.

NOTE

A star will appear on the Family Page next to anyone with a match in the FamilyFinder report.

11

Correcting Information in Family Tree Maker

In a perfect world, each piece of information you placed in your Family Tree file would be accurate and you would never need to make any changes. However, since no one is infallible when entering data, Family Tree Maker offers ways to undo family relationships, check your spelling, and delete individuals. In this chapter, you'll learn how to:

- Use the spelling checker
- Undo a marriage
- Delete individuals from your Family Tree file
- Check for data entry errors

Working with the Family Tree Maker Spelling Checker

While we'd all like to think we don't make mistakes, there are times when, in typing the details of a will or the place of birth based on a faded record, you might not always get the spelling correct. However, you might not notice the error right away.

Checking Spelling in the Entry Screens

You can ask Family Tree Maker to spell check all the notes and text items in a book from the entry screens and report windows.

1. Click on **Edit**. The Edit menu will appear.

2. Click on **Spell Check All**. The Spell Check dialog box will open and Family Tree Maker will move to the first Notes screen and highlight the first word not found in the dictionary.

CAUTION

It is important to understand that the spelling checker is going to go through all of your Notes screens when it is launched in this manner. Depending on how many notes you have, this could take some time.

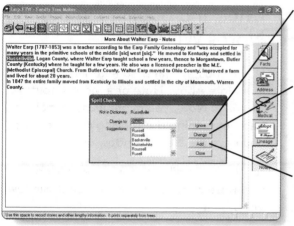

3a. **Click** on **Ignore** to ignore the word and move on in the spell check.

OR

3b. **Click** on **Change** to replace the highlighted word with the word listed in the Change to field.

OR

3c. **Click** on **Add** to place the highlighted word in the dictionary.

NOTE

If the word in the Change field is not the one you want, you can click on one of the other words in the Suggestions list to replace the word in the Change field.

TIP

If the dictionary does not supply you with the appropriate choice, you can type in the word in the Change to field and then click on the Change button. Family Tree Maker will make the change.

NOTE

When the spelling checker highlights a word, it does not necessarily mean that the word is misspelled. It simply means that the word is not yet in the spelling checker's dictionary. This will be true of most surnames and place names that may be entered in the Notes section. Those used frequently should be added to the dictionary to prevent false hits in the spell check.

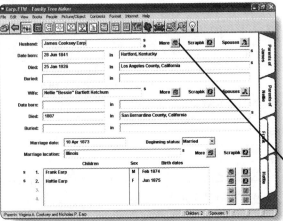

Checking Spelling in the Notes Windows

When you have finished entering the details in a More About Note or a More About Marriage Note, you might want to make a habit of running the spelling checker while you have the Notes window open.

1. In the Family Page window, **click** on the **More button**. The More About window will appear.

2. Click on the **Notes button**. The More About Notes window will appear.

3. Click on **Edit**. The Edit menu will appear.

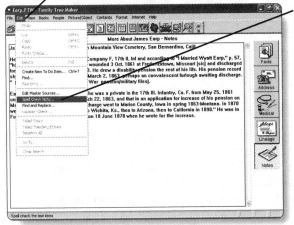

4. Click on **Spell Check Note**. The spelling checker will start.

NOTE

When the spelling checker is finished with that specific Note, it will ask whether you want to check the other Notes in the family file. Clicking on Yes will run the spelling checker on all the other Notes in the family file. Clicking on No will end the spelling check.

Untying the Marriage Knot

As you continue with your research, you might discover that your information about a marriage is inaccurate. This is especially likely when you get into areas where you have multiple generations of the same name (for instance, John Smith, son of John Smith). Family Tree Maker includes options for undoing a marriage if you discover that the individuals you listed as married are not the correct two people.

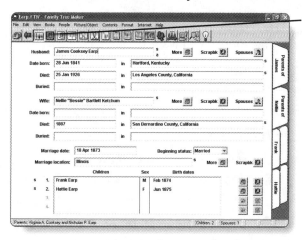

1. **Click** on the **Family Page button**. The Family Page window will appear.

2. **Click** on the **Index of Individuals button**. The Index of Individuals dialog box will open.

3. **Type** the **name** of the individual for whom you need to untie a marriage.

4. **Click** on the correct **individual** in the list, if he or she is not already selected.

5. **Click** on **Go to Family Page**. The Family Page window for the selected individual will appear.

NOTE

You might need to select the appropriate spouse. See Chapter 3, "Family Tree Maker for Beginners," for a quick review on how to do this.

6. **Click** in the **Wife (or Husband) field** for the spouse you want to detach.

7. **Click** on **People**. The People menu will appear.

8. **Move** the **mouse pointer** to Fix Relationship Mistakes. The Fix Relationship Mistakes menu will appear.

9. **Click** on **Detach Spouse**. Family Tree Maker will open a message box, verifying that you want to detach the spouse.

10. **Click** on **OK** to confirm the change.

NOTE

Any children associated with the marriage will remain with the spouse who was not detached.

TIP

Be sure to read the final message box that confirms the detach of the child or children. It includes steps to reattach the individual. You can also find detailed steps for attaching a child in "Linking Children to Their Parents" in Chapter 12, "Fixing Relationships & Duplicates."

Removing People from Your Family File

Detaching a spouse removes the individual from the marriage, but it does not remove the individual from your Family Tree file. However, you might discover that you have an individual or group that needs to be deleted completely from the database.

Deleting One Person

When you discover a single individual who should be removed from the database, you can delete that person in the Family Page window.

1. **Click** on the **Family Page button**. The Family Page window will appear.

> ### TIP
>
> The individual you want to delete must be listed in the Family Page window. Use the Index of Individuals or Find Individual options, if necessary, to select the person you want to delete.

2. **Click** in the **name field** for the individual you want to delete.

3. **Click** on **People**. The People menu will appear.

4. **Click** on **Delete Individual**. A message box will appear, verifying that you want to delete the individual.

5a. **Click** on **Yes** if you want to delete the individual.

OR

5b. **Click** on **No** if you do not want to delete the individual.

Deleting a Group of People

If you want to delete a group of individuals, you can select them via the Tree views and the Custom Report. The group of individuals to be deleted must be visible on the tree or report in order for you to delete them as a group.

1. **Click** on a **Tree button**. The selected Tree menu will appear.

2. **Click** on a **Tree style**. The appropriate Tree window will appear.

NOTE

You can use the Custom Report to select those individuals who are not necessarily related by blood or descent.

NOTE

Look at the primary person on the report. It is important to verify that the primary person and those related to that person and displayed on the report are indeed the individuals you wish to delete. If the person isn't the individual you want, you can use the Index of Individuals to select a new person.

3. **Click** on the **Index of Individuals button**. The Index of Individuals dialog box will open.

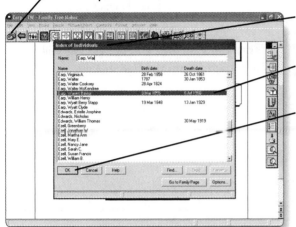

4. **Type** the **name** of the desired individual in the Name field.

5. **Click** on the correct **individual** in the list, if he or she is not already selected.

6. **Click** on **OK**. The Index of Individuals dialog box will close and the newly selected individual will be displayed in the report.

TIP

Some of the reports allow you to include siblings. You will learn more about this in Chapter 13, "Looking at the Tree Reports in Family Tree Maker."

---

7. **Click** on **People**. The People menu will appear.

8. **Click** on **Delete Individuals in Ancestor Tree**. A message box will appear, verifying that you do indeed want to delete the individuals from your Family File. The actual wording of this menu item will differ, depending on the type of report or Tree you selected.

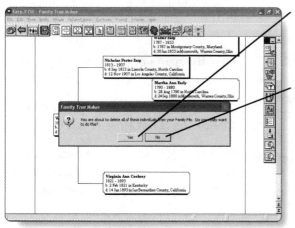

9a. **Click** on **Yes**. The individuals will be deleted from the Family File.

OR

9b. **Click** on **No**. The individuals will not be deleted from the Family File.

CAUTION

Deleting individuals from the Family File becomes permanent as soon as you move on to something else in the program. You have one chance directly after removing the individuals to bring them back using the Undo feature found under the Edit menu. If you are not familiar with this feature, create a backup of your family file before deleting anyone. You can learn more about backup files in Chapter 21, "Working with GEDCOM Files and Other Family Files."

Checking the Family File for Errors

Family Tree Maker offers you three different ways to scan your Family File for errors. One is automatic, another runs a scan when you request it, and the third is a report of the errors that Family Tree Maker has found.

Data Entry Checking

Family Tree Maker offers a feature that works automatically after it is turned on. This data entry checking feature will let you know when you have entered what Family Tree Maker thinks is a questionable date or name error.

1. **Click** on **File**. The File menu will appear.

2. **Move** the **mouse pointer** to **Preferences**. The Preferences menu will appear.

3. **Click** on **Error Checking**. The Error Checking dialog box will open.

4. **Click** on the **Name errors check box**. Family Tree Maker will check for name errors.

5. **Click** on the **Unlikely birth, death, and marriage dates check box**. Family Tree Maker will check for date errors.

6. **Click** on **OK**. The Error Checking dialog box will close.

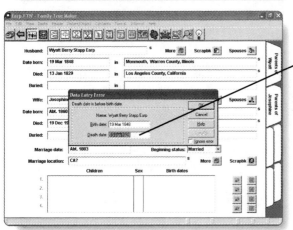

NOTE

When you type in a date that doesn't coincide with the other dates for an individual or family, Family Tree Maker will open a Data Entry Error message box to point out the problem. From this box you can type in the correct date and then click the OK push button to make the change. This is talked about in detail in the next section "Using the Find Error Command."

Using the Find Error Command

The Find Error command is like a spelling checker for the dates that have been entered. It identifies the errors and then allows you to fix or skip each error.

1. **Click** on the **Family Page button**. The Family Page window will appear.

NOTE

You must be in the Family Page in order to use the Find Error command. You will find it is disabled in other views in the program.

---

2. **Click** on **Edit**. The Edit menu will appear.

3. **Click** on **Find Error**. The Find Error dialog box will open.

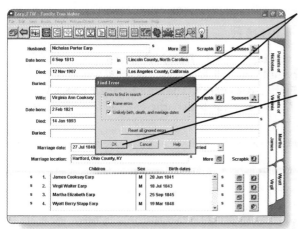

4. Select the **errors** for which you want to search. You can search for name errors and/ or unlikely birth, death, and marriage dates by selecting the appropriate check box.

5. Click on **OK**. Family Tree Maker will search your Family File for errors. When an error is found, you will have several options.

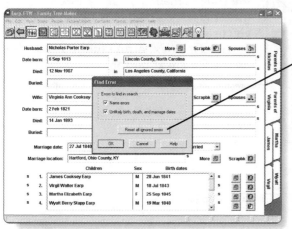

NOTE

The Reset all ignored errors button allows you to overwrite the Ignore Error check box you will be introduced to in the next set of steps.

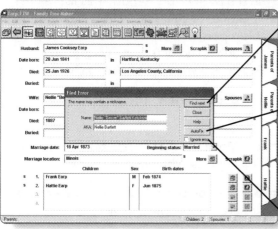

6a. Click on the **Find next button**. Family Tree Maker will bypass the error and find the next one.

OR

6b. Click on the **AutoFix button**. Family Tree Maker will change the error based on where it thinks the information should be placed.

OR

6c. Click on the **Ignore error check box**. Family Tree Maker will ignore the error now (and in the future, if you want it to).

NOTE

If you turn on the Ignore error check box, Family Tree Maker will ignore the error each time you run Find Error until you click on the Reset all ignored errors button at the start of the Find Error search. The Ignore error check box can be used to have Family Tree Maker bypass those idiosyncrasies unique to the names or dates you are entering.

TIP

If you selected AutoFix in error, or if the change made by Family Tree Maker is not correct, click on Undo. If you use the Undo feature, you will not move to the next error until you click on the Find next button.

Working with the Data Errors Report

From time to time it is a good idea to run the Data Errors Report. This lists all the potential errors that Family Tree Maker identifies in your Family File. After printing this report, you can take time to read through it and determine what in your Family File you might need to change.

1. Click on **View**. The View menu will appear.

2. Move the **mouse pointer** to Reports. The Reports submenu will appear.

3. Click on **Data Errors**. The Data Errors Report window will appear.

4. Click on an **individual** to highlight that person in the list. Notice the potential error.

5. Double-click on the **individual** to edit his or her information. The Individual Facts Card for that individual will appear.

6. Correct the **error** in the Individual Facts Card.

7. Click on **OK** to return to the Data Errors Report to work on the next error. The Data Errors Report will reappear.

NOTE

If you have corrected all the errors in the Data Errors Report, when you click on OK as above, you may get a message box telling you that the person does not belong in the current view. Answering Yes will take you to the Family Page for that person. Answering No will take you back to the Data Error report.

12

Fixing Relationships & Duplicates

Sometimes after you have imported a relative's GEDCOM or data from World Family Tree, you will discover that you have some duplicate individuals. At other times, you might find that you need to adjust the relationship between a child and the parents. In this chapter, you'll learn how to:

- Link children to their parents
- Detach a child from the wrong parents
- Link individuals by marriage
- Merge duplicates
- Search and replace

Fixing Relationships

There will be times when it will be necessary to change the relationships between the individuals in your Family File. Family Tree Maker recognizes that, as your research progresses, there will be times when you will discover an error in how you have connected individuals in a family structure.

Linking Children to Their Parents

You might discover that you already have a child and his or her parents entered in your Family File, but you did not realize they were related when you originally entered them. It's easy to link children to parents in Family Tree Maker.

1. Click on the **Family Page button**. The Family Page window will appear.

2. Click on the **Index of Individuals button**. The Index of Individuals dialog box will open.

> ### TIP
>
> You can also access the Index of Individuals dialog box by pressing F2.

3. Click on the **individual** you want to include on the Family Page.

4. Click on **OK**. The Family Page window will show the new individual.

> ### NOTE
>
> You need to select one of the parents of the child you wish to add.

5. Click on **People**. The People menu will appear.

6. Move the **mouse pointer** to **Fix Relationship Mistakes**. The Fix Relationship Mistakes menu will appear.

7. Click on **Attach Child**. The Select the Child dialog box will open.

8. Type the **name** of the individual you want to add as a child.

9. Click on the **name** of the individual in the list.

10. Click on **OK**. A message box will appear, verifying that you want to attach the individual as a child on the Family Page.

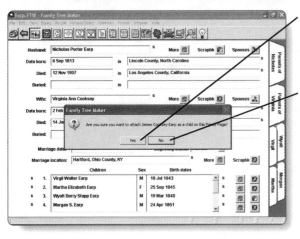

11a. Click on **Yes**. The child will be added to the Family Page.

OR

11b. Click on **No**. The child will not be added to the Family Page.

NOTE

If the child in question had siblings from another relationship, Family Tree Maker will ask whether or not the siblings should also be associated with the new parents.

Detaching a Child from the Wrong Parents

If you discover that a child has been linked to the wrong parents, you can easily detach the child from that family. This will not delete the child from the Family File.

1. **Press F2**. The Index of Individuals dialog box will open.

2. **Type** the **name** of one of the parents in the Name field.

3. **Click** on the correct **name** in the list.

4. **Click** on **Go to Family Page**. The family will be displayed in the Family Page window.

5. Click on the **child** you want to detach in the Children list.

6. Click on **People**. The People menu will appear.

7. Move the **mouse pointer** to **Fix Relationship Mistakes**. The Fix Relationship Mistakes menu will appear.

8. Click on **Detach Child**. A message box will appear, asking if you want to detach the siblings of the selected individual as well.

9a. Click on **Yes**. The siblings of the child will also be detached.

OR

9b. Click on **No**. The siblings of the child will not be detached.

NOTE

The final message box will verify that you do indeed wish to detach the child from the family. Answering yes will detach the child. Answering no will leave the child where he or she is in the family.

Linking Individuals by Marriage

Unlike typing in the names of two spouses in the Family Page, the steps for linking two previously entered individuals require picking one of the individuals out of a list.

1. Click on **View**. The View menu will appear.

2. Click on **Index of Individuals**. The Index of Individuals dialog box will open.

3. Click on the **individual** you want as one of the spouses.

4. Click on **Go to Family Page**. The Family Page window will appear.

NOTE

There must be a place for the new spouse to go. That means that in the Family Page, the spouse field must be empty. If the individual in question already has a spouse, you need to use the Spouses button to add the spouse. See Chapter 3, "Family Tree Maker for Beginners," for a quick review of how to do that.

5. Click on **People**. The People menu will appear.

6. Move the **mouse pointer** to **Fix Relationship Mistakes**. The Fix Relationship Mistakes menu will appear.

7. Click on **Attach Spouse**. The Select the spouse dialog box will open.

8. Click on the **name** of the individual you want to select as the spouse.

9. Click on **OK**. A message box will appear, asking if you're sure you want to make the selected individual the spouse.

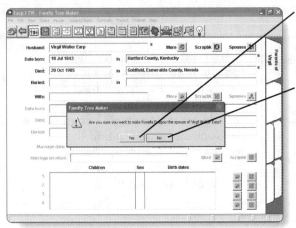

10a. **Click** on **Yes**. The spouse will be attached.

OR

10b. **Click** on **No**. The spouse will not be attached.

Fixing Duplicates

Often, when you are adding information from a fellow researcher, you will end up with duplicate individuals in your Family File. Sometimes the duplication is the result of entering an individual twice.

Fixing Duplicate Files for the Same Person

Family Tree Maker offers a method to merge individuals that looks not only at the name of the individuals, but also at additional information, such as family relationships and dates of events.

1. **Click** on the **Family Page button**. The Family Page window will appear.

2. Click on **People**. The People menu will appear.

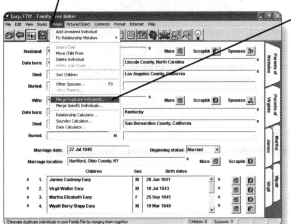

3. Click on **Merge Duplicate Individuals**. A message box will appear, reminding you to back up your file before you merge duplicate individuals.

TIP

You should make it a practice to save your family file as a back up before you do anything major to it. For more on saving back up files, see Chapter 21, "Working with GEDCOM Files and Other Family Files."

4. Click on **OK**. The Merge Duplicate Individuals dialog box will open.

5. Click on **Display merge report**. The Merge Individuals Report window will appear.

NOTE

If Family Tree Maker cannot find duplicates, a message box will appear, telling you that none were found.

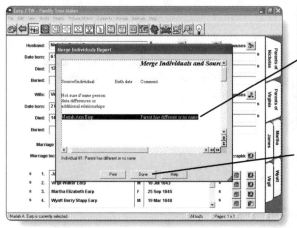

TIP

You can click on an individual in the list to get some additional information about the differences between the two possible duplicates.

6. Click on **Done**. The Merge Duplicate Individuals dialog box will reappear.

7. Click on **Merge matching information**. The Merge Individuals dialog box will open.

NOTE

Family Tree Maker automatically merges two individuals with the same information. You are given the option of whether to merge two individuals with differing information.

8a. Click on **Merge**. The two individuals will be merged.

OR

8b. Click on **Don't merge**. The two individuals will not be merged.

TIP

After you have merged individuals, Family Tree Maker will remind you that you can undo the merge, provided that you do it before you exit the program. Click on OK to close the message box, and then print out and read through the Merge Report to make sure everything was merged correctly.

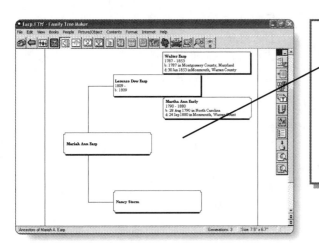

TIP

In addition to viewing the Merge Report, be sure to view the individuals in the various views to verify that everything is correct. If it's not, you can use the Undo option to undo the merge. You must do this before exiting Family Tree Maker.

Merging Specific Individuals

There are times when you will want total control over the individuals you wish to select for merging. You gain this control using the Merge Specific Individuals menu option.

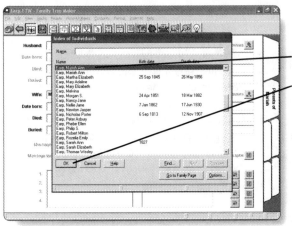

1. Press F2. The Index of Individuals dialog box will open.

2. Select one **individual** you wish to merge.

3. Click on **OK**. The Family Page will open.

4. Click on **People**. The People menu will appear.

5. Click on **Merge Specific Individuals**. The Select the individual who is the same as dialog box will open.

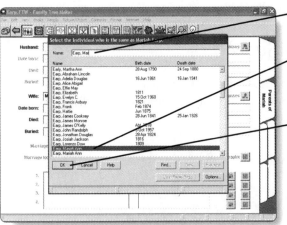

6. Enter the **name** of the second individual in the Name field.

7. Click on the **name** of the person with whom you wish to merge the first individual.

8. Click on **OK**. A message box will appear, verifying that the individuals should be merged.

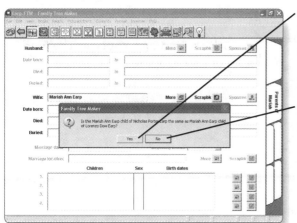

9a. **Click** on **Yes**. The two individuals will be merged and the Merge Individuals dialog box will open.

OR

9b. **Click** on **No**. The two individuals will not be merged.

NOTE

You will have another opportunity to verify that the two individuals are the same. If they are, then click on the Merge button. If they are not, click on the Cancel button.

Using Global Find and Replace

You may discover that you have consistently misspelled a word or phrase. The Find and Replace feature allows you to have Family Tree Maker search for the wrong word or phrase and replace it with the correct one.

1. **Click** on the **Family Page button**. The Family Page will appear.

2. Click on **Edit**. The Edit menu will appear.

3. Click on **Find and Replace**. The Find and Replace dialog box will open.

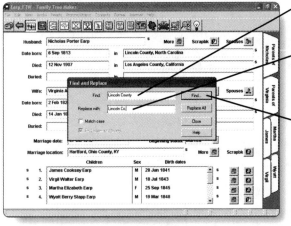

4. In the Find field, **enter** the **word or phrase** you want to find.

5. In the Replace with field, **type** the **word or phrase** with which you want to replace it.

6. Click on **Find**. The Find and Replace dialog box will show the first match.

7a. Click on **Replace All**. Family Tree Maker will replace all occurrences of the Find word with the Replace with word.

OR

7b. Click on **Replace**. Family Tree Maker will replace just that particular occurrence of the Find word with the Replace with word.

OR

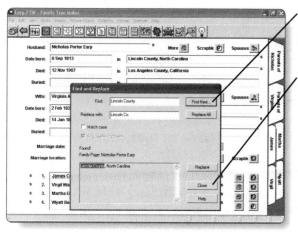

7c. Click on **Find Next**. Family Tree Maker will ignore the current occurrence and look for the next match.

8. Click on **Close**. Family Tree Maker will close the Find and Replace dialog box.

Part III Review Questions

1. How can you access the Index of Individuals? *See "Using Quick Search by Name" in Chapter 10*

2. What are the ways you can arrange the Index of Individuals? *See "Rearranging the Index" in Chapter 10*

3. What are the other ways you can search for an individual in your Family File? *See "Using the Find Individual Feature" in Chapter 10*

4. How can you search for online research using Family Tree Maker? *See "Working with the FamilyFinder Center" in Chapter 10*

5. What are the two ways you can run the spell checker in Family Tree Maker? *See "Working with the Family Tree Maker Spelling Checker Feature" in Chapter 11*

6. How can you delete an individual from your Family File? *See "Deleting One Person" in Chapter 11*

7. What are the three ways you can check your Family File for errors? *See "Checking the Family File for Errors" in Chapter 11*

8. How can you link a previously entered child to previously entered parents? *See "Linking Children to Their Parents" in Chapter 12*

9. What two ways can you merge duplicate individuals in your Family File? *See "Fixing Duplicates" in Chapter 12*

10. How can you do a global find and replace of a word or phrase? *See "Using Global Find and Replace" in Chapter 12*

PART IV

Getting to Know Family Tree Maker Trees and Reports

13

Looking at the Tree Reports in Family Tree Maker

After you have entered information about your family into Family Tree Maker, it is natural for you to want to display that information in different formats. Family Tree Maker offers a number of different trees that will show you ancestors, descendants, or both for a selected individual. In this chapter, you'll learn how to:

- Display Ancestor Trees
- Display Hourglass Trees
- Display Descendant Trees
- Display All-in-One Trees
- Share the Standard Pedigree Tree
- Enhance the Tree views

Displaying Ancestor Trees

The Ancestor Trees allow you to see how many direct line generations you have been able to carry your research back from a selected individual. Family Tree Maker offers four different versions of the Ancestor Tree.

Creating Fan Charts

The Fan Chart of an Ancestor Tree begins with the selected individual. It then displays all the ancestors: parents, grandparents, great-grandparents, and so on. You can control how the chart looks and how many generations to include.

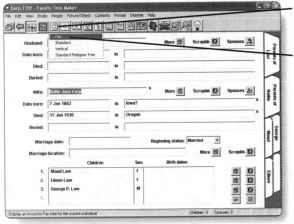

1. **Click** on the **Ancestor Tree button**. The Ancestor Tree menu will appear.

2. **Click** on **Fan**. The Fan Chart will appear.

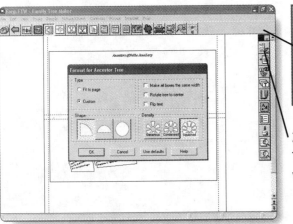

TIP

Family Tree Maker allows you to change the format of the chart using the toolbar along the right side of the tree.

3. **Click** on the **Format button**. The Format for Ancestor Tree dialog box will open.

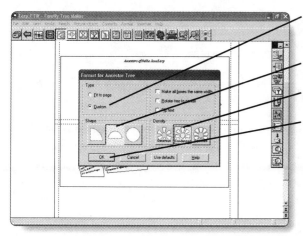

4. **Select** the **Custom radio button**. All the options will be enabled.

5. **Select** the **shape** of the Fan Chart.

6. **Select** the **density** of the Fan Chart.

7. **Click** on **OK**. The Format for Ancestor Tree dialog box will close and your changes will be saved.

NOTE

Throughout this chapter, you will examine all the different toolbar buttons as you learn about each tree.

Creating a Pedigree Chart

The pedigree chart is the standard chart used by genealogists. This chart is a road map of your direct lineage and usually displays from four to six generations per page.

1. **Click** on the **Ancestor Tree button**. The Ancestor Tree menu will appear.

2. **Click** on **Standard**. The Standard Pedigree Chart will appear.

3. Click on the **Format button**. The Tree Format for Ancestor Tree dialog box will open.

4. Select the **type of Ancestor Tree** you want to display.

5. Select the **type of connections** you want to use in the chart. The chart's boxes will be moved closer together or further apart, depending on the type of connections you select.

NOTE

The Layout options are only active when you select the Custom type.

TIP

When you select the Book layout type, you can elect to have each tree centered on the page.

6. Click on **OK**. The Tree Format for Ancestor Tree dialog box will close and your changes will be saved.

7. **Click** on the **Zoom Out button**. You will see more of the tree.

Rearranging the Standard Ancestor Chart

While the Ancestor Tree is a standard form, better known as a pedigree chart, many researchers find that they like to customize the chart. In addition to the methods mentioned earlier, you also can move individual boxes or a complete lineage using your mouse and the keyboard.

NOTE

You must be in the Custom format to be able to rearrange the tree.

1a. **Click** on the **individual** whose lineage you want to move. The individual and his or her lineage are selected.

OR

1b. **Hold** down the **CTRL key** while you **click** on the **individual** you want to move. Only that individual will be selected.

2. **Drag** the **mouse** to the new location. The individual or the selected lineage will be moved elsewhere on the chart that you have selected.

TIP

Remember that when you are dragging the mouse, it is necessary to hold down the left mouse button or the left mouse button and the CTRL key to achieve the desired effect.

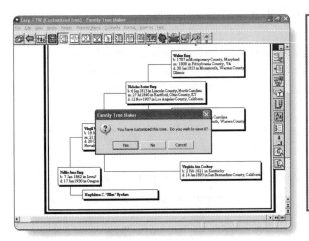

TIP

If changes have been made to the tree and you select another view, such as the Family Page, or another report, you will be asked if you want to save the custom view. Click Yes to save the custom view. Click No if you don't want to save the custom view. Clicking Cancel will return you to the tree you changed.

3. **Type** the **name** you want to give the custom tree. This will be the name of the tree as it appears in the Save View As list.

4. **Click** on **OK**. The Save View As dialog box will close and the tree will be saved.

NOTE

For more on using trees and reports you have saved using the Save As option, see Chapter 24, "Enhancing Your Family History Book."

Creating a Vertical Ancestor Tree

The Vertical Ancestor Tree is a box-style chart. It starts at the bottom of a page or set of pages and goes up, showing the ancestors of the selected individual.

1. **Click** on the **Ancestor Tree button**. The Ancestor Tree menu will appear.

2. **Click** on **Vertical**. The Vertical Ancestor Tree will appear.

TIP

You can change what information is included in the boxes for each of the individuals.

---

3. **Click** on the **Items to Include button**. The Items to Include in Ancestor Tree dialog box will open.

4. **Click** on an **item** in the Available items list.

5. **Click** on the **Inclusion button**. The Options dialog box will open.

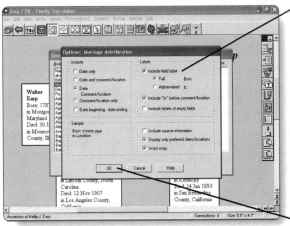

6. **Click** on the **options** for the selected item. A check mark will appear next to the options selected.

TIP

If you want to see how the options will affect the name, look at the sample shown in the bottom left section of the dialog box.

7. **Click** on **OK**. The Options dialog box will close and the item will appear in the The boxes in your tree contain these items list.

NOTE

The choices in the Options dialog box will vary depending on the item you selected from the Available items list.

8. **Click** on an **item** in the The boxes in your tree contain these items list. The item will be selected.

9. **Click** on the **Move up or Move down button**. The item will be moved to a new position.

10. **Click** on **OK**. The changes will be applied to the Vertical Ancestor Tree.

NOTE

The order in which the items appear in the The boxes in your tree contain these items list is the order in which they will appear in the boxes of the tree.

Including Siblings on Trees

Once in a while you might want to get a good overall view of your data with more than just the direct ancestral lineage. Taking advantage of the option to include siblings is one way to do that. Before beginning these steps, make sure you have the Vertical Ancestor Tree open.

NOTE

While this example concentrates on the Vertical Ancestor Tree, this option is available for all of the Ancestor Tree formats, as well as for the Standard Hourglass Tree.

---

1. **Click** on the **Options button**.
The Options for Ancestor Tree dialog box will open.

2. **Click** on the **Include siblings check box** for the siblings you wish to add to the Vertical Ancestor Tree. A check mark will appear in the selected box.

3. **Click** on **OK**. The Options for Ancestor Tree dialog box will close.

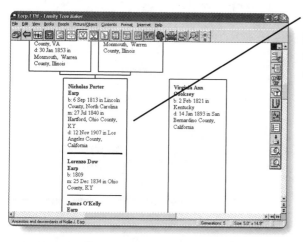

Notice how the changes affect the overall look of the Vertical Ancestor Tree, especially if you have elected to include the siblings for everyone on the tree.

Sharing the Standard Pedigree Tree

If you are sharing with genealogists who have been researching their family tree for some time, they might feel more comfortable with a printed standard pedigree tree. This tree resembles the forms that genealogists have been using for many years, including having blank spaces for relatives to add information and return to you. This is a good tree to take with you when researching at a library or other repository.

1. Click on the **Ancestor Tree button**. The Ancestor Tree menu will appear.

2. Click on **Standard Pedigree Tree**. The Standard Pedigree Tree will appear.

TIP

The Standard Pedigree Tree allows you to send a tree to a fellow researcher or relative so that he or she can supply you with information you might not have known.

NOTE

When you are in the Standard Pedigree Tree, Family Tree Templates are disabled. You will learn more about this feature of the tree reports in "Enhancing Your Tree with Templates" in Chapter 15.

3. Click on the **Box, Line, & Border Styles button**. The Styles for Ancestor Tree dialog box will open.

4. Click on the **Borders tab**. The Borders options will appear in the dialog box.

5. Select a **border style** from the choices shown. The border will be selected.

TIP

If you find when printing your trees or reports with a color printer that there is a background printing out, you can get rid of it by making sure the Background color option in the Borders section is set to none.

6. Click on **OK**. The Styles for Ancestor Tree dialog box will close and changes will be made to the Standard Pedigree Tree.

NOTE

While many of the same style and option changes can be made to the Standard Pedigree Chart, it is best to keep it as close to the original as possible, since this is a recognized report to almost all genealogists.

Displaying Hourglass Trees

The Hourglass Tree allows you to view not only the ancestors but also the descendants of the selected individual. The selected individual is in the center with the ancestors opening above and the descendants opening below, looking much like an hourglass.

Working with Fan Format

Like other fan-styled trees, the Hourglass Tree in fan format takes advantage of the fan shape. Keep in mind that with a large lineage, the fan style will use up a lot of paper when you print it.

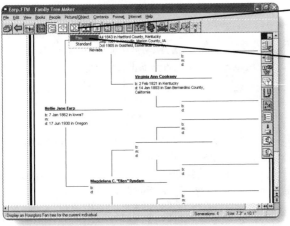

1. **Click** on the **Hourglass Tree button**. The Hourglass Tree menu will appear.

2. **Click** on **Fan**. The fan format of the Hourglass Tree will appear.

TIP

If the primary individual isn't the one that you want, you can use the Index of Individuals dialog box, available in the View menu or by pressing F2, to select a different individual. See Chapter 10, "Searching Your Family Tree File," to review how to do this.

---

3. **Click** on the **Number of Generations button**. The # of Generations to Show dialog box will open.

4. **Use** the **arrows** to select the number of generations of ancestors and descendants desired.

5. **Click** on **OK**. The # of Generations to Show dialog box will close and changes will be applied to the Hourglass Tree.

Working with Standard Format

The standard format of the Hourglass Tree uses a box chart. The boxes can be as large or as small as you want, depending on the information you include. Remember that the more information you elect to include, the fewer individuals will fit on a given page.

1. **Click** on the **Hourglass Tree button**. The Hourglass Tree menu will appear.

2. **Click** on **Standard**. The standard format of the Hourglass Tree will appear.

TIP

You can determine the events and comments included in each box; simply click on the Items to Include button.

3. **Click** on the **Box, Line, & Border Styles button**. The Styles for Hourglass Tree dialog box will open.

4a. **Click** on the **Boxes tab** to access style and color options for the boxes.

OR

4b. **Click** on the **Borders tab** to access style and color options for the border of the tree.

OR

4c. **Click** on the **Lines tab** to access style and color options for the lines connecting the boxes.

NOTE

Each of these sections uses buttons and drop-down menus to make the options available. It is through these options that you change the look and feel of the chart.

Displaying Descendant Trees

There will be times when you want to view the descendants of a given ancestor. Some research projects will require tracing the children and grandchildren. Descendant Trees allow you to see these in an easy-to-read format.

Creating a Standard Tree

As with the other trees you have looked at, there is a standard format of the Descendant Tree. This standard tree is often known as a box chart. It details the descendants of a selected individual.

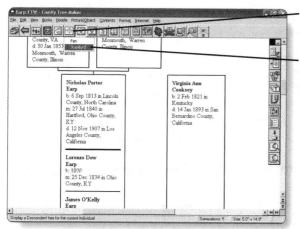

1. **Click** on the **Descendant Tree button**. The Descendant Tree menu will appear.

2. **Click** on **Standard**. The standard format of the Descendant Tree will appear.

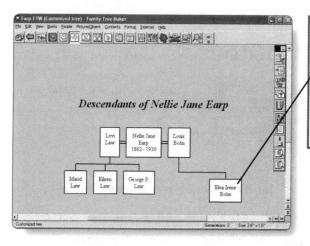

TIP

You can rearrange the shape of the Standard Descendant Tree by clicking and dragging, as you did with the Standard Ancestor Tree earlier in this chapter.

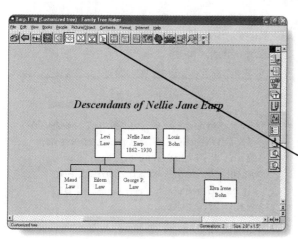

Creating an Outline Tree

When you're working with the descendants of a given individual, Family Tree Maker offers an outline, or indented, tree. Each generation is indented, making it easy to distinguish each generation from the others.

1. **Click** on the **Outline Descendant Tree button**. The Outline Report will appear.

2. Click on the **Format button**. The Tree Format for Outline Descendant Tree dialog box will open.

NOTE

This dialog box allows you to change the indent character as well as the size and spacing.

3. Click on **OK**. The Tree Format for Outline Descendant Tree dialog box will close.

Displaying All-in-One Trees

There will be times when you will want to view all the individuals in your database. Family Tree Maker makes this possible with the All-in-One Tree.

Creating an All-in-One Tree

An All-in-One Tree is easily created because Family Tree Maker does all the hard work.

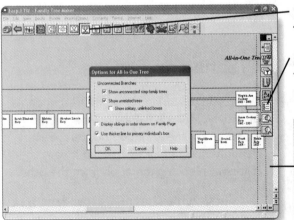

1. Click on the **All-in-One Tree button**. The All-in-One Tree will appear.

2. Click on the **Options button**. The Options for All-in-One Tree dialog box will open.

NOTE

The dotted lines you see on the All-in-One Tree display the page margins. The All-in-One Tree will require multiple pages when printed, and those pages will then need to be taped together.

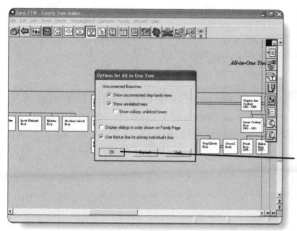

TIP

The Unconnected Branches check boxes allow you to include or exclude unconnected lines that have been entered in your database.

3. **Choose** your desired **settings** and **click** on **OK**. The Options for All-in-One Tree dialog box will close.

Setting Display Size

Because the All-in-One Tree displays all the individuals in your database, its size can be cumbersome. Customizing the display size can make it easier to understand the true scope of this view.

1. **Click** on the **Zoom Out button**. The All-in-One view will zoom in.

2. **Use** the **scroll bar** to move the All-in-One Tree to see the boxes not currently on the screen.

NOTE

To read the information for a given individual, it may be necessary to click on the Zoom In button a couple of times.

TIP

You can also use the View menu to select the Zoom options. To see the entire All-in-One Tree, choose Size to Window.

Pruning the Display

In addition to excluding the unrelated trees, you can control the number of generations included in your tree.

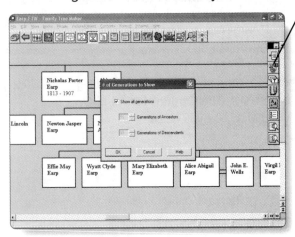

1. Click on the **Number of Generations button**. The # of Generations to Show dialog box will open.

2. Click on the **Show all generations check box** to clear it.

3. Use the **arrows** in the Generations of Ancestors field to select the number of generations of ancestors you want to show.

4. Use the **arrows** in the Generations of Descendants field to select the number of generations of descendants you want to show.

5. Click on **OK**. The # of Generations to Show dialog box will close and the changes will appear on the tree.

TIP

A quick way to change the number of generations of ancestors or descendants is to double click on the number of generations to highlight it and then type in the new number.

Enhancing Tree Views

There are different ways to enhance the appearance of the different trees. With colors and different box styles, you can make different lineages or genders stand out. The Descendant Tree report is one that benefits from these types of enhancements.

Emphasizing Relationships

With line styles and colors, you can make a particular relationship clearer on your tree.

1. **Click** on the **Box, Line, & Border Styles button**. The Styles dialog box will open.

> ### NOTE
>
> The exact name of the Styles dialog box will vary, depending on what type of tree you are enhancing.

2. **Click** on the **Lines tab**. The Lines tab will move to the front.

3. **Click** on the **Highlight the relationship between check box** to select or deselect it. A check mark will appear when you select this option and will disappear when you deselect it.

4. **Click** on the **Change button** to change one of the individuals currently selected. The Index of Individuals dialog box will open and will include a list of only those individuals already included in the tree.

5. Click on the desired **individual** in the list. The selected individual will be highlighted.

6. Click on **OK**. The Index of Individuals dialog box will close.

7. Click on the **Line color down arrow**. The Line color drop-down menu will appear.

8. Click on a **color**. The color will be selected.

9. Click on **OK**. The Styles dialog box will close and your changes will be saved.

Adding a Background Image

There is nothing more interesting than enhancing the overall appearance of your tree. This can be done effectively by placing a picture in the background.

1. Click on the **Picture/Object** menu. The Picture/Object menu will appear.

2. Click on **Tree Background Picture**. The Background Picture dialog box will open.

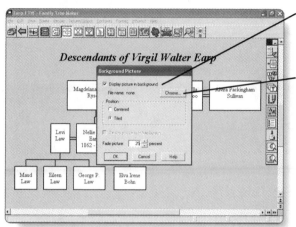

3. **Click** on the **Display picture in background check box**. The option will be selected.

4. **Click** on the **Choose button**. The Insert Picture window will open so you can select a picture.

NOTE

At this point you can make changes to the selected picture. This is discussed in more detail in Chapter 17, "Creating a Scrapbook."

TIP

After selecting a digitized picture, you might want to fade the picture so that it does not make reading the tree difficult. The smaller the number in the **Fade Picture** field, the more faint the picture will appear behind the chart, making the chart easier to read.

5. **Click** on **OK**. The Background Picture dialog box will close and the picture will appear in the background of the report.

14

Working with Specialty Reports and the Research Journal

In addition to its many trees, Family Tree Maker also includes a number of other reports that allow you to understand what you have in your database and how the individuals might be related. In this chapter, you'll learn how to:

- Create a Custom Report
- Create a Kinship Report
- Create an Address Report
- Create a Birthday Report
- Use the Research Journal

Creating a Custom Report

Just as the name implies, Custom Reports allow you to control the individuals and information included in the reports.

1. **Click** on the **Report button**. The Report window will appear.

2. **Click** on the **Report Format button**. The Report Format dialog box will open.

3. **Click** on **Custom Report** in the Select a format for your report list.

4. **Click** on **OK**. The Report Format dialog box will close.

Adding Items to Include in Your Report

The Custom Report might not have in it the information you want to include. However, this report is easy to adjust.

1. **Click** on the **Items to Include button**. The Items to Include in Report dialog box will open.

2. In the Available items list, **click** on an **item** that you want to include.

3. **Click** on the **Inclusion button**. The Options dialog box might open, depending on the item you've chosen to include.

NOTE

Not all of the Items to Include options will have detailed options. When nothing needs to be selected, the Options dialog box will not open.

4. Select the desired **options**. A check mark will appear next to the options you have selected.

5. Click on **OK**. The Options dialog box will close and the items you selected will be included in the Each row of your report will contain list.

Choosing Individuals to Include in Your Report

You might want to limit the individuals appearing in the report if you do not want to show your entire database. You can do this individually or by relationship.

1. Click on the **Individuals to Include button**. The Include dialog box will open.

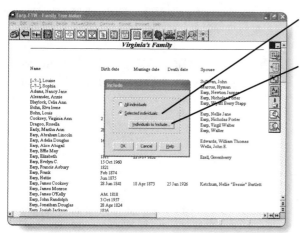

2. Click on the **Selected individuals** radio button. The option will be selected.

3. Click on the **Individuals to Include button**. The Individuals to Include dialog box will open.

4. In the Available individuals list, **select** the **individual** you want to include.

5. **Click** on the appropriate **Inclusion button.** The individual you selected (and his or her ancestors or descendants, if applicable) will be moved to the You have included these individuals list.

NOTE

There are four major Inclusion buttons. The > button tells Family Tree Maker to include the single highlighted individual. The >> button will include all the individuals. The Ancestors button will include the ancestors of the highlighted individual. The Descendants button will include the descendants and their spouses of the highlighted individual.

TIP

To learn how to use the Find button to determine the individuals you want to include in the list, see Chapter 22, "Working with the Custom Report."

6. **Click** on **OK.** The Individuals to Include dialog box will close and your changes will be saved.

Creating a Title and Footnote

If you will be supplying this report to others, you might want to give it a title and include a footnote that will appear on each page.

1. **Click** on **Contents**. The Contents menu will appear.

2. **Click** on **Title & Footnote**. The Title & Footnote for Report dialog box will open.

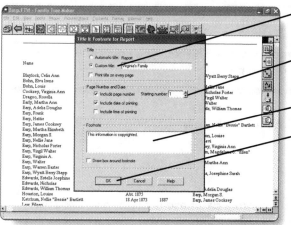

3. **Click** on a **radio button** to select the appropriate title option.

4. **Select** the desired **page number, date, and time options**.

5. **Type** a **footnote** in the Footnote field.

6. **Click** on **OK**. The Title & Footnote for Report dialog box will close.

Adjusting Column Widths

Sometimes, in an effort to fit as much information in a report as possible, it is necessary to adjust the column widths.

1. **Click** on **Format**. The Format menu will appear.

2. **Click** on **Maximum Width for each Column**. The Maximum Width for Each Column dialog box will open.

3a. **Click** on the **Set widths automatically radio button**. The option will be selected.

OR

3b. **Click** on the **Choose widths manually radio button**. The option will be selected.

4. If you chose to adjust the widths manually, **adjust** the **width and spacing** for each column.

TIP

Pay close attention to the total report width. This lets you know how much space your columns will take up on the page.

---

5. **Click** on **OK**. The Maximum Width for Each Column dialog box will close.

Sorting Reports

One benefit of putting this information into a database is that it gives you the ability to manipulate the data after it has been entered. You can sort the report based on the columns included.

1. **Click** on **Format**. The Format menu will appear.

2. **Click** on **Sort Report**. The Sort Report dialog box will open.

3. From the Sort by drop-down menu, **select** the **first column** by which you want to sort.

4a. **Click** on the **Ascending radio button** to sort in ascending order.

OR

4b. **Click** on the **Descending radio button** to sort in descending order.

5. From the Then by drop-down menu, **select** the **second column** by which you want to sort, if desired.

6. **Click** on **OK**. The Sort Report dialog box will close.

Creating a Kinship Report

Kinship Reports help you determine just how individuals in your database are related. The people making up several generations might be related in more than one way.

1. **Click** on **Format**. The Format menu will appear.

2. **Click** on **Report Format**. The Report Format dialog box will open.

3. Click on **Kinship - Relationship Only** in the Select a format for your report list. The Kinship - Relationship Only report will be selected.

4. Click on **OK**. The Report Format dialog box will close.

TIP

Remember that you can change the primary individual. Press F2 or click on the Index of Individuals button to open the Index of Individuals and select the person you want as the primary individual.

Working with Address and Birthday Reports

Whether you find yourself the keeper of addresses for the family association or you just want to print out a report of birthdays so you will be sure to send cards, Family Tree Maker kept you in mind.

Creating an Address Report

If you have taken advantage of the Address More About option for living individuals, you can print out a report with those addresses.

1. Open the **Report Format dialog box**, as you did in the previous section, "Creating a Kinship Report."

2. Click on **Address** in the Select a format for your report list. The Address Report will be selected.

3. Click on **OK**. The Report Format dialog box will close.

TIP

You can determine which individuals are included in the Address Report. Simply click on the Individuals to Include button.

NOTE

You might have some unexpected individuals in your report. Individuals can "inherit" an address if one has been entered for a parent or spouse.

Creating the Birthday Report

Thanks to the Birthday Report, you no longer need to look through all the pages of your living family members to find birthdays. The Birthday Report can display the birthdays of all the living individuals in your database, or it can show just those you want to select.

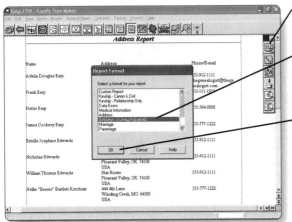

1. Click on the **Report Format button**. The Report Format dialog box will open.

2. Select the **Birthdays of Living Individuals** report from the Select a format for your report list.

3. Click on **OK**.

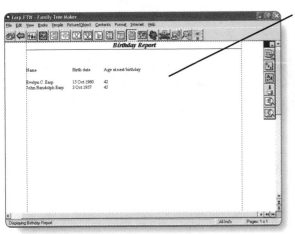

The Report Format dialog box will close and the Birthday Report will be displayed.

NOTE

Family Tree Maker omits anyone with a death date and anyone who is more than 120 years old.

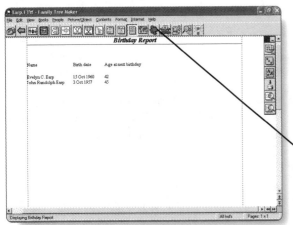

Using the Research Journal

The Research Journal offers a means for tracking your past research and for making notes on future research.

1. Click on the **FamilyFinder Center button**. The FamilyFinder Center window will appear.

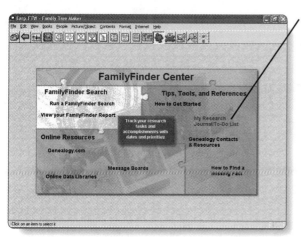

2. **Click** on **My Research Journal/To-Do List**. The Research Journal screen will appear.

Creating a New To-Do Item

The Research Journal allows you to record a list of items that still need to be accomplished in your research. By using the Research Journal, you no longer need to remember these items, just simply look at your to-do list before your next research trip.

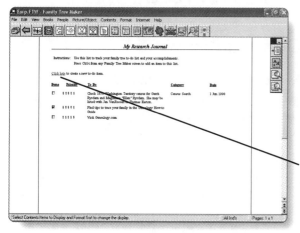

1. **Click** on the **Click here to create a new to-do item** link to add a To-Do item. The New To-Do Item dialog box will open.

2. **Enter** a **description** of what you want to accomplish in the To-Do field.

3. **Click** on the **arrows** in the Priority field to select a priority. For a low priority leave this number at 1 or 2. A high priority would be a 4 or 5.

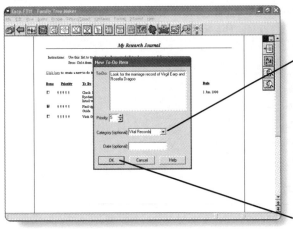

TIP

You can use the Category field to organize your To-Do items under categories such as Census or Church Records, which you define.

4. Type in a **date** in the Date field. This is the date by which the task needs to be completed.

5. Click on **OK**. The New To-Do Item dialog box will close.

Viewing Done or Not Done Items

The Research Journal is your road map of the research you have done and the research that still must be accomplished. There will be times when you will want to see it all, and other times when you will want to see only what you have done or what is left to do.

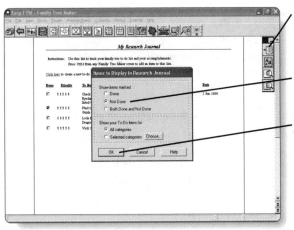

1. Click on the **Items to Display button**. The Items to Display in Research Journal dialog box will open.

2. Select a **Show items marked option**. The item will be selected.

3. Click on **OK**. The Items to Display in Research Journal dialog box will close.

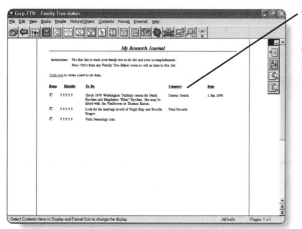

The Research Journal will reflect the changes in the items listed based on whether the To-Do item has been done or is still pending.

Viewing Items for a Certain To-Do Category

Another way to affect the format of the Research Journal is through the To-Do categories. Usually based on resources or repositories, the To-Do categories allow you to narrow the focus of the report to just those entries for the selected category or categories.

1. **Click** on the **Items to Display button**. The Items to Display in Research Journal dialog box will open.

2. **Click** on the **Both Done and Not Done option**. All items, whether done or not, will be included in the Research Journal.

3. **Click** on the **Choose button**. The Categories to Include dialog box will open. This dialog box is the same as many of the others you've seen. You simply select items from the Available list and place them in the other list.

4. Click on **OK**. The Categories to Include dialog box will close, saving the list of selected categories as they appear in the Show items from these categories list.

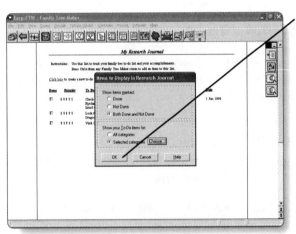

5. Click on **OK**. The Items to Display in Research Journal dialog box will close and the Research Journal will reflect your changes.

NOTE

The two To-Do items already in the Research Journal that refer to the Genealogy How-to Guide and Visit Genealogy.com will appear regardless of the choices you make in terms of what items to display in the Show your To-Do items section. While you can mark them as Done, you cannot delete them as you can delete the items you enter.

TIP

If you want to delete a To-Do item that you have created, you can do so by clicking on the item so that it is highlighted and then pressing the Delete key.

Working with the Genealogy How-To Guide

Whether you are just beginning or you have been involved for a while in researching your family history, there will be times when you will have questions about where to go with your research.

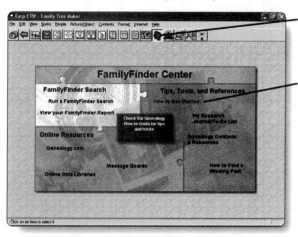

1. **Click** on the **FamilyFinder Center button**. The FamilyFinder Center window will appear.

2. **Click** on **How to Get Started**. The Genealogy "How-To" Guide window will appear.

3. **Click** on an **item of interest**. Further instructions will appear.

4. **Click** on the **Close button** in the upper-right corner of the window. The Genealogy "How-To" Guide window will close.

15

Viewing and Printing Reports and Trees

Now that you have learned how to enter information and view some of the reports and trees, you're probably very interested in learning how to format them and print them out. In this chapter, you'll learn how to:

- View the tree you want to print
- Customize the view of the tree
- Change the print setup
- Print the tree
- Save the tree

Viewing the Tree You Want to Print

Family Tree Maker assumes that the tree or report you are interested in is the one on the screen, so you need to display the tree to print it.

1. **Click** on the **tree view** you want to print. A menu might appear, depending on which tree view you select.

2. If a menu does appear, **click** on the **tree type** you want to print. The tree will appear.

Customizing the View

After you have displayed the tree you want to print, you can fine-tune the text style, font, and size. The changes will display on the screen so you can make sure the tree looks the way you want before you send it to the printer.

1. **Click** on the **Text Font & Style button**. The Text Font, Style, & Size dialog box will open.

NOTE

The complete name of the dialog box will depend on the tree or report that you have selected.

Changing the Text Font

One wonderful aspect of computers and modern printers is that you can be creative with the fonts you use. You can go from formal to fun.

1. **Click** on an **item** in the Items to format list.

2. **Click** on the **Font down arrow**. The Font drop down menu will appear.

3. **Click** on the **font** you want to use. The font will be selected and the Font drop-down menu will close.

NOTE

Use the scroll bar to view the list of fonts. Please note that the list of fonts available will depend on the number of fonts you have installed on your computer.

TIP

If you use the keyboard arrow keys to move through the list of fonts, you will see a sample of each font in the Sample box.

Working with Text Style

In order to make things stand out, you might want to change the style of the text. For instance, you might decide that you want to italicize the dates to call attention to them.

1. **Select** an **item** to format from the Items to format list.

2. **Click** on the **Style down arrow**. The Style drop-down menu will appear listing the styles available based on the font previously selected.

3. **Click** on the desired **style**. The style will be selected and the drop-down menu will close.

NOTE

If you want more than one item to have this style, press the Ctrl key and click on the additional items in the Items to format list. Then select the style from the Style drop-down menu.

Working with Text Size

Family Tree Maker has developed a number of default sizes for the fonts used in reports. You can change these if you want to, but in some cases it might make your report much larger.

1. **Select** an **item** to format from the Items to format list.

2. **Click** on the **Size down arrow**. The Size drop-down menu will appear.

3. **Click** on the desired **size**. The size will be selected and the drop-down menu will close.

TIP

You can change the font, size, and style of an item all at once. Just select the item from the Items to format list and make your desired changes.

Working with Text Color

If you are going to a family reunion or some other gathering where you want your chart to look extra special, you will want to take advantage of the color options Family Tree Maker offers.

1. Select an **item** to format from the Items to format list.

2. Click on the **Color down arrow**. The Color drop-down menu will appear.

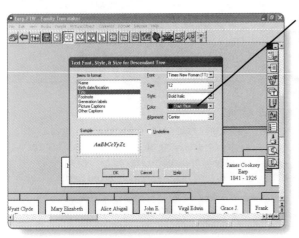

3. Click on the desired **color**. The color will be selected and the drop-down menu will close.

NOTE

Remember if you are selecting colors to enhance the chart, you must be printing to a color printer for these enhancements to appear.

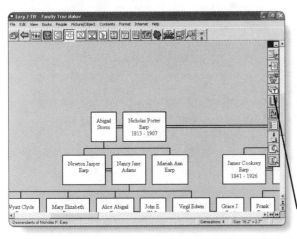

Enhancing Your Tree with Templates

Another way to truly enhance your family tree chart is through the use of templates. Templates offer creative borders and other artwork to all of the individuals in the chart with just a simple selection. The Family Tree Templates offer researchers an easy way to create beautiful trees with little effort.

1. Click on the **Family Tree Templates button**. The Family Tree Templates dialog box will appear.

TIP

The Family Tree Templates can also be accessed by clicking on the Format menu and selecting Family Tree Templates from the menu that appears.

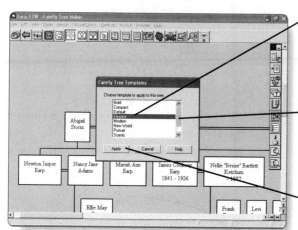

2. **Click** on the **template choice**. That template will be selected.

NOTE

Be sure to see all the templates by using the scroll bar on the right of the list.

3. **Click** on the **Apply button**. The selected template will be applied to the family tree chart.

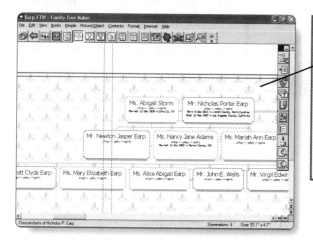

TIP

If you do not like the look of the template, and you have not done anything else, such as zooming in or out to view the template better, you can use the CTRL+Z keyboard shortcut to undo the changes to the report or click on the Edit menu and select.

NOTE

If you did make other changes to the report after applying the template and you would like to remove the template, simply follow the above steps and select Default from the template choices.

Printing the Tree

After you have formatted your tree the way you want, it is time to print it.

1. **Click** on **File**. The File menu will appear.

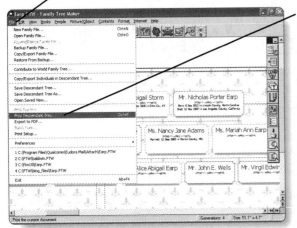

2. **Click** on **Print Tree**. The Print Tree dialog box will open.

NOTE

The actual name of the Print Tree dialog box will vary depending on the tree selected.

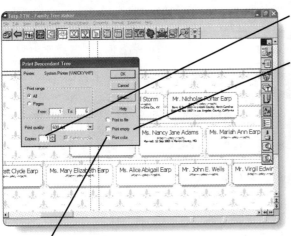

3. In the Copies field, **enter** the **number of copies** you want to print.

4. **Select** the **Print empty check box** to print an empty tree.

TIP

Some of the trees or reports may not offer the Print empty check box. When it is unavailable, it will be grayed out.

5. **Select** the **Print color check box** to print the tree in color, if you have a color printer.

NOTE

Printing an empty tree is an excellent way to have needed forms when you are on a research trip.

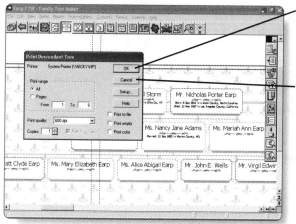

6a. **Click** on **OK**. The tree will be sent to the printer.

OR

6b. **Click** on **Cancel**. The tree will not be printed.

Saving the Tree in PDF Format

Many of us would like to save our trees in a format that we can share either on disk or through e-mail with relatives or fellow researchers. Due to the nature of the formatting of these trees, this requires a special method of saving found in Portable Document or PDF format. The PDF format is a good way to save a tree file to have printed professionally for a family reunion as well.

1. **Click** on the **File menu**. The File menu will appear.

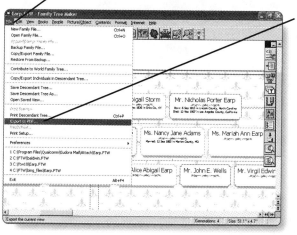

2. **Click** on **Export to PDF**. The Export tree dialog box will open.

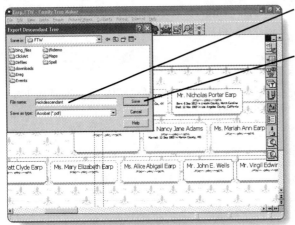

3. Type in the **name of the file** in the **File name field.**

4. **Click** the **Save button**. The file will be saved.

NOTE

The Save as type option will default to PDF, the Portable Document Format created by Adobe. Remember that when sharing this type of file with others, they must have the Adobe Acrobat Reader installed on their system to read the file. If you wish to view saved files on your computer, you must also have the reader, which you can download by visiting the Adobe Web site (http://www.adobe.com).

16

Creating Genealogy Style and Genealogical Source Reports

After you have entered all your information, you will want to share it with family members and other researchers. The Genealogy Style Reports are one of the best ways to do this. In this chapter, you'll learn how to:

- Select a genealogy style
- Include sources as endnotes in reports
- Format the report
- Locate conflicting data
- Create a Bibliography Report
- Create a Documented Events Report

Using Genealogy Style Reports

Genealogy Reports in Family Tree Maker are narrative reports containing genealogical information, basic facts, and biographical details. These are the most common formats you see in published family histories.

Working with Register Format

The Register format gets its name from the journal that devised it, *The New England Historic Genealogical Register*. This report lists individuals in order of descent.

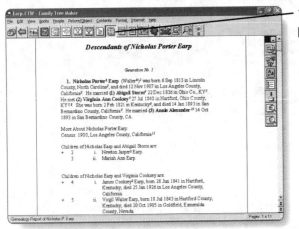

1. **Click** on the **Genealogy Report button**. The Genealogy Report will appear.

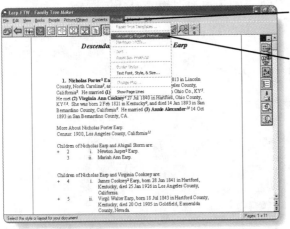

2. **Click** on **Format**. The Format menu will appear.

3. **Click** on **Genealogy Report Format**. The Genealogy Report Format dialog box will open.

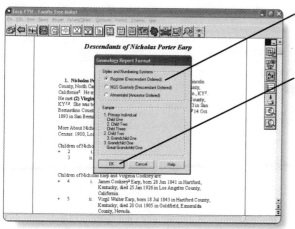

4. Click on the **Register (Descendant Ordered) radio button**. The option will be selected.

5. Click on **OK**. The Genealogy Report Format dialog box will close.

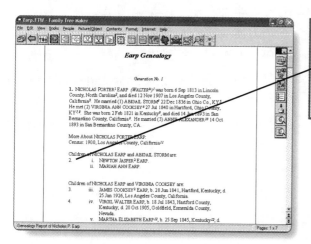

NOTE

The Register format assigns an identifying number to those who have offspring.

Working with NGS Quarterly Format

The NGSQ format also displays individuals in order of descendants. It was named after the *National Genealogical Society Quarterly,* the journal of the National Genealogical Society.

TIP

The *National Genealogical Society Quarterly* style requires that the names of months be spelled out completely. If you want to adhere to this standard in your report, you will need to change your Date preferences. To review this, see "Changing the Date Format" in Chapter 3, "Family Tree Maker for Beginners."

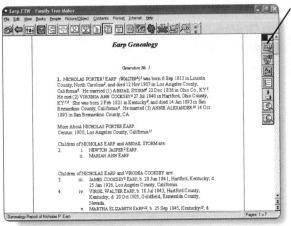

1. Click on the **Format button**. The Genealogy Report Format dialog box will open.

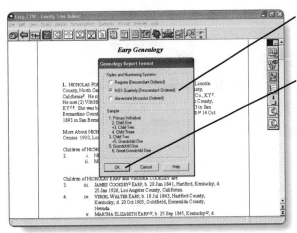

2. Click on the **NGS Quarterly (Descendant Ordered) radio button**. The option will be selected.

3. Click on **OK**. The Genealogy Report Format dialog box will close.

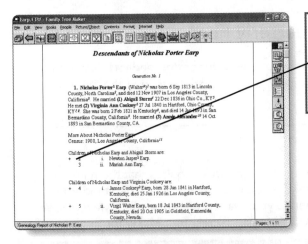

NOTE

The NGSQ format assigns a number to each individual and assigns a plus sign to those with offspring.

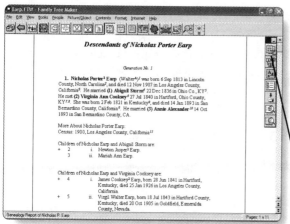

Using the Ahnentafel Report

Ahnentafel is a German word that means "ancestor table" or "family table." This report lists individuals in an ancestral order. This is the opposite of the other two reports.

1. Click on the **Format button**.
The Genealogy Report Format dialog box will open.

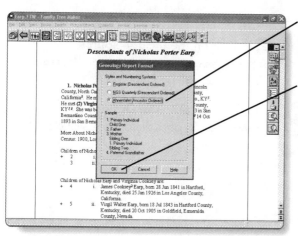

2. Click on the **Ahnentafel (Ancestor Ordered) radio button**. The option will be selected.

3. Click on **OK**. The Genealogy Report Format dialog box will close.

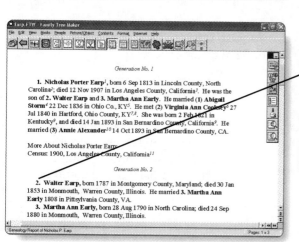

NOTE

The Ahnentafel style assigns the first individual the number 1. His or her father is number 2 and his or her mother is number 3. Men are always even numbers and women are always odd numbers.

Using Endnotes

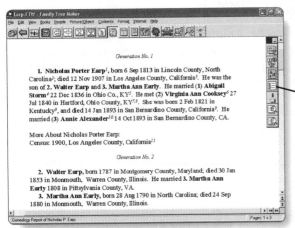

Genealogy Style Reports include source citations. These can be included in the body of the report or they can be printed as endnotes.

1. **Click** on the **Options button**. The Options for Genealogy Report dialog box will open.

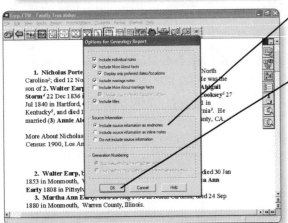

2. **Click** on the **Include source information as endnotes radio button**. The option will be selected.

3. **Click** on **OK**. The Options for Genealogy Report dialog box will close.

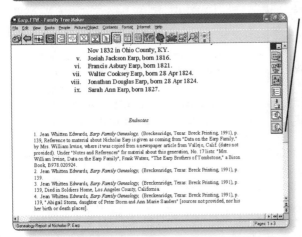

4. **Use** the **scroll bar** to scroll to the bottom of the report.

NOTE

The endnotes are the source citations, or footnotes, you learned about in Chapter 5, "Documenting Sources." When they are placed at the end of a report, they are referred to as endnotes.

Formatting the Report

In addition to the different styles of reports, there are other items that need to be considered, such as page numbering and the type of notes to include.

Adjusting Title and Page Numbering

Family Tree Maker has default settings for the title and page number, but you can change these settings.

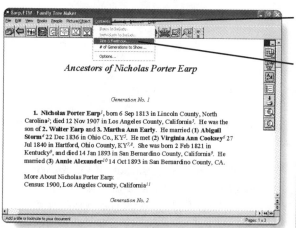

1. **Click** on **Contents**. The Contents menu will appear.

2. **Click** on **Title & Footnote**. The Title & Footnote for Genealogy Report dialog box will open.

NOTE

All of the reports allow for title and footnote options. The title of this dialog box will vary depending on which type of report or tree you are using.

3a. **Click** on the **Automatic title radio button**. The option will be selected.

OR

3b. **Click** on the **Custom title radio button**. The cursor will move to the empty field, where you will type the title as you want it to display in the report.

4. In the Page Number and Date section, **click** on the **page number and date options** you want to set.

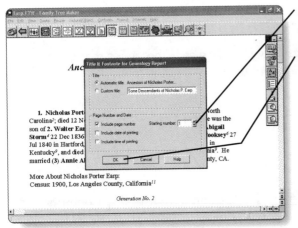

5. Use the **up and down arrows** to change the starting page number.

6. Click on **OK**. The Title & Footnote for Genealogy Report dialog box will close.

Changing the Number of Generations

As you can do with the trees, you can control the number of generations that are included in the Genealogy Report.

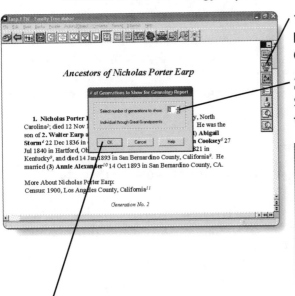

1. Click on the **Number of Generations button**. The # of Generations to Show for Genealogy Report dialog box will open.

2. Use the **up and down arrows** in the Select number of generations to show field to adjust the number.

TIP

The number in the Select number of generations to show field is highlighted when the dialog box is opened, so you can just type the number of generations to include in the report if you prefer not to use the up and down arrows.

3. Click on **OK**. The # of Generations to Show for Genealogy Report dialog box will close.

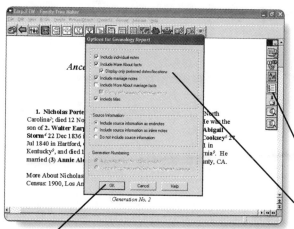

Including Notes and Other Options

In Chapter 7, "Using More About Notes," you learned to include family stories. These stories can be included in printed reports.

1. **Click** on the **Options button**. The Options for Genealogy Report dialog box will open.

2. **Click** on the **notes check boxes** for the options you want to set.

3. **Click** on **OK**. The Options for Genealogy Report dialog box will close.

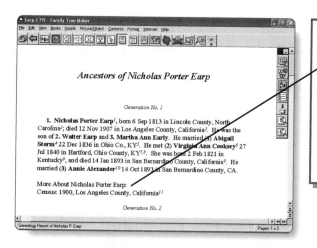

TIP

It is a good idea to read through the report to see if the notes are appropriate and should be included. Even if you have not opened the Options dialog box, some notes will be included because Family Tree Maker has note options turned on by default.

Locating Conflicting Facts

Family Tree Maker allows you to enter duplicate facts. This is by design, because you will find dates in your research that conflict with each other and you want to record each of them. Family Tree Maker also lets you conduct a search based on these conflicting facts.

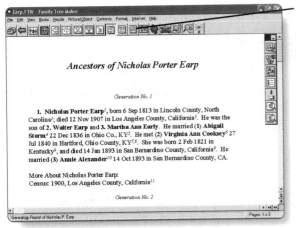

1. **Click** on the **Report button**. The last report opened will appear.

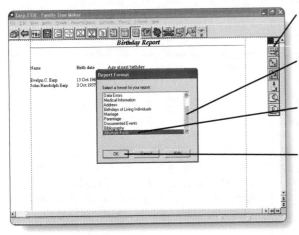

2. **Click** on the **Format button**. The Report Format dialog box will open.

3. **Scroll down** until you reach the bottom of the Select a format for your report list.

4. **Click** on **Alternate Facts**. The option will be selected.

5. **Click** on **OK**. The Report Format dialog box will close.

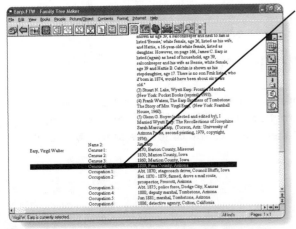

6. **Click** on an **individual** from the report. The individual will be selected.

7. **Click** on **View**. The View menu will appear.

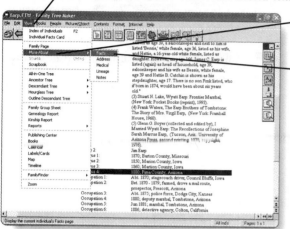

8. **Move** the **mouse pointer** to More About. The More About menu will appear.

9. **Click** on **Facts**. The More About Facts window will appear.

> ### NOTE
>
> You can now view the facts for the individual.

Creating a Bibliography Report

A bibliography is a list of books and sources. These are the sources you have used to compile your Family Tree file. A Bibliography Report is a useful reference tool.

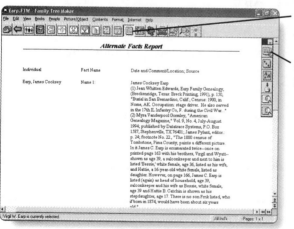

1. **Click** on the **Report button**. The Report will appear.

2. **Click** on the **Format button**. The Report Format dialog box will open.

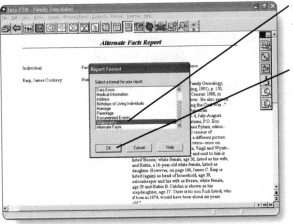

3. **Click** on **Bibliography** in the Select a format for your report list. The option will be selected.

4. **Click** on **OK**. The Report Format dialog box will close.

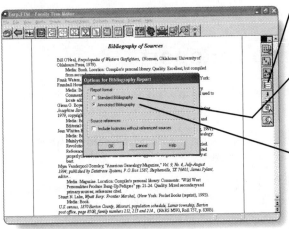

5. **Click** on the **Options button**. The Options for Bibliography Report dialog box will open.

6a. **Click** on **Standard Bibliography** to create a standard bibliography.

OR

6b. **Click** on **Annotated Bibliography** to create an annotated bibliography.

NOTE

The annotated bibliography includes the full source citation and comments by the researcher about the source.

Creating a Documented Events Report

Understanding how you came to the conclusions you did in your Family Tree file is usually directly related to the sources used. The Documented Events Report is a clear list of the individuals and events you have documented.

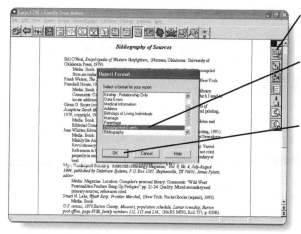

1. **Click** on the **Format button**. The Report Format dialog box will open.

2. In the Select a format for your report list, **click** on **Documented Events**. The option will be selected.

3. **Click** on **OK**. The Report Format dialog box will close.

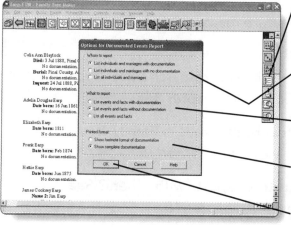

4. **Click** on the **Options button**. The Options for Documented Events Report dialog box will open.

5. **Click** on the desired **Whom to report radio button**. The option will be selected.

6. **Click** on the desired **What to report radio button**. The option will be selected.

7. **Click** on the desired **Printed format radio button**. The option will be selected.

8. **Click** on **OK**. The Options for Documented Events Report dialog box will close.

Part IV Review Questions

1. What four types of Ancestor Trees can you display? See *"Displaying Ancestor Trees" in Chapter 13*

2. Which Descendant Tree indents the individuals? *See "Creating an Outline Tree" in Chapter 13*

3. How do you view a complete All-in-One Tree? *See "Setting Display Size" in Chapter 13*

4. How do you select the items to include in a Custom Report? *See "Adding Items to Include in Your Report" in Chapter 14*

5. How can you record plans for future research? *See "Using the Research Journal" in Chapter 14*

6. Where can you turn for guidance in your research? *See "Working with the Genealogy How-To Guide" in Chapter 14*

7. How do you alter the overall feel to the trees in Family Tree Maker? *See "Customizing the View" in Chapter 15*

8. How do you share your various tree reports with others? *See "Saving the Tree in PDF Format" in Chapter 15*

9. What three types of Genealogy Reports are available? *See "Using Genealogy Style Reports" in Chapter 16*

10. Can you create a bibliography of the sources used in your research? *See "Creating a Bibliography Report" in Chapter 16*

PART V

Publishing Your Family History

17

Creating a Scrapbook

Using present technology, it is possible to create beautiful reports and enhance them by adding scanned and digitized photographs. Family Tree Maker calls these reports scrapbooks. In this chapter, you'll learn how to:

- Use a scrapbook
- Insert images into a scrapbook
- Enter information about scrapbook items
- Rearrange scrapbook objects
- Edit pictures or objects
- Search for objects
- Share your scrapbook

Using the Scrapbook

The scrapbook is where you can work with digitized files such as scanned photographs. There are scrapbooks for individuals and for marriages.

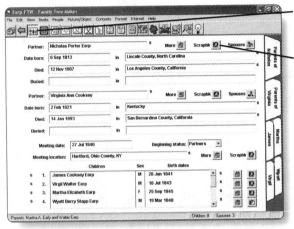

1. Click on the **Family Page button.** The Family Page window will appear.

2. Click on the **Scrapbk button.**

The Individual Scrapbook window will appear. Each frame can hold a digitized photo, video clip, sound clip, or other object.

Inserting Scrapbook Objects

While most of the items you will work with will be scanned photographs, Family Tree Maker does support video and sound clips and OLE (*Object Linking and Embedding*) objects.

Using Graphics Images

Scanning photographs helps to preserve them, and they can then be included in the reports you print from Family Tree Maker. But first you need to import the image files.

1. Click on **Picture/Object**. The Picture/Object menu will appear.

2. Click on **Insert Picture from File**. The Insert Picture dialog box will open.

TIP

It is also possible to scan the picture directly into the scrapbook. Click on Insert Picture from Scanner/Camera. Remember, though, that images can take up a great deal of space on your hard drive. For scanned images, it is recommended that you set the resolution to a maximum of 200 DPI (*Dots Per Inch*). This will produce a good picture and keep the file size down at the same time.

3. Use the **Look in drop-down menu** to locate the folder that holds the images.

4. Click on the desired **image**. The image will be selected.

5. Click on **Open**. The Insert Picture dialog box will close and the picture will appear in the Edit Picture dialog box.

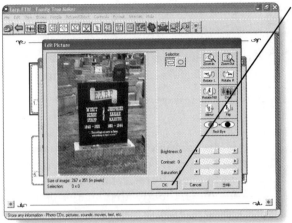

6. Click on **OK**. The Edit Picture dialog box will close.

Using Sound Clips

There is something fascinating about hearing the voice of a relative. Family Tree Maker offers a way of including sound clips in the scrapbook.

1. Click on **Picture/Object**. The Picture/Object menu will appear.

2. Click on **Insert Object**. The Insert Object dialog box will open.

3. Click on the **Create from File radio button**. The option will be selected.

4. Click on the **Browse button**. The Browse dialog box will open.

5. **Use** the **Look in drop-down menu** to locate the proper folder.

6. **Click** on the desired **file**. The file will be selected.

7. **Click** on **Open**. The Browse dialog box will close.

8. **Click** on the **Display As Icon check box**. The option will be selected.

9. **Click** on **OK**. The Insert Object dialog box will close.

Using OLE Objects

Object Linking and Embedding (OLE) allows you to launch another program from within Family Tree Maker. You might want to do this so you can open a word-processing file to display a detailed family story.

1. **Click** on **Picture/Object**. The Picture/Object menu will appear.

2. **Click** on **Insert Object**. The Insert Object dialog box will open.

TIP

If you click on the Create New radio button, you can select an object type from the list that appears. Then click on OK and the program will start.

3. Click on the **Create from File radio button**. The option will be selected.

4. Click on the **Browse button**. The Browse dialog box will open.

5. Use the **Look in drop-down menu** to select the desired folder.

6. Click on the desired **file**. The file will be selected.

7. Click on **Open**. The Browse dialog box will close.

8. Click on the **Display As Icon check box**. Family Tree Maker will insert an icon in the scrapbook.

9. Click on **OK**. The Insert Object dialog box will close.

Entering Information About Scrapbook Objects

To help you identify your scrapbook objects, Family Tree Maker offers a More About screen for each scrapbook entry.

1. **Click** on the **More About button** for the selected scrapbook item. The More About Picture/Object dialog box will open.

2. **Type** a **caption** in the Caption field.

3. **Type** a **category** in the Category field.

> ### TIP
>
> Plan ahead before you use the Category field. Family Tree Maker allows you to categorize your scrapbook objects, making them easier to search.

4. **Type** in the **date of origin** if known in the Date of origin field.

5. **Type** a **description** for the object in the Description field.

6. **Select** the desired **preferred check box(es)**. The option(s) will be selected.

TIP

Remember that while Family Tree Maker can display sound clips and OLE objects, in a printed report you will only get the digitized images.

---

7. **Click** on the **Include in show check box** if you want the object to display when you play the scrapbook.

8. **Click** on the **Include in printed Scrapbook check box** if you want the object to display in the printed scrapbook.

9. **Click** on **OK**. The More About Picture/Object dialog box will close.

Rearranging Scrapbook Objects

There might be a time when you want the items or objects in the scrapbook to display in a particular order that's different from the way you originally entered them.

Moving Objects

One way to rearrange the objects inserted in a scrapbook is to move them.

1. **Click** on the **object** you want to move. The object will be selected.

2. **Click** on **Edit**. The Edit menu will appear.

3. **Click** on **Cut Picture/Object**. The picture will be moved to the Clipboard.

4. **Click** in the **frame** where you want to place the object.

5. **Click** on **Edit**. The Edit menu will appear.

6. **Click** on **Paste Picture/Object**. The object will be pasted in the new position.

Copying Objects

You can copy and paste a scrapbook item from the scrapbook of one individual to that of another.

1. **Click** on the **object** you want to copy.

2. **Click** on **Edit**. The Edit menu will appear.

3. **Click** on **Copy Picture/Object**. The object will be copied to the Clipboard.

4. **Click** on the **Index of Individuals button**. The Index of Individuals dialog box will open.

5. **Click** on the **individual** into whose scrapbook you want to paste the object. The individual will be selected.

6. **Click** on **OK**. The new individual's scrapbook will open.

7. **Click** on the **frame** where you want to place the object.

8. **Click** on **Edit**. The Edit menu will appear.

9. **Click** on **Paste Picture/Object**. The copied object will be placed in the scrapbook.

Enhancing Your Images

Family Tree Maker has included the ability to rotate, crop, mirror, and flip images. You also can adjust color and brightness and remove red eye from digitized photos.

Cropping an Image

There are times when the scanned image has more than you wish to include in your reports. By cropping the image, you can limit the part of the picture that will be used in your scrapbook.

1. **Click** on **Picture/Object**. The Picture/Object menu will appear.

2. **Click** on **Edit**. The Edit Picture dialog box will open.

TIP

Instead of the Edit Picture dialog box, you may get a message box suggesting you get the original before editing it. It is always best to edit the original to preserve the quality of the image. Clicking yes will open the Insert Picture dialog box in the directory where that file is stored with that file already selected. Just click on the Open push button and the Edit Picture dialog box will open.

3. **Click and drag** the **mouse pointer** to highlight the area of the image you want to keep. The area will be selected.

4. **Click** on the **Crop button**. The picture will be cropped.

TIP

You can undo the changes by clicking on the Cancel button. The Edit Picture dialog box will close, and no changes will be made.

---

5. **Click** on **OK**. The Edit Picture dialog box will close.

Adjusting Color and Brightness

There are times when the image has shadows or the image is not as clear as you had hoped. Through adjusting the color, brightness, and saturation, it might be possible to better see the individuals in the picture, bringing them somewhat out of the shadow.

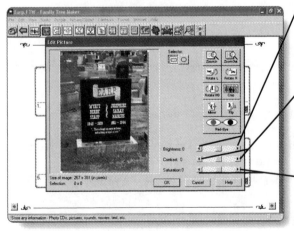

1. **Click** on the **right** or **left arrow** for the **brightness**. The brightness level will change: brighter to the right and darker to the left.

2. **Click** on the **right** or **left arrow** for the **contrast**. The contrast level will change: more contrast to the right and less to the left.

3. **Click** on the **right** or **left arrow** for the **saturation**. The color of the picture will change: more color to the right and more like a black and white picture to the left.

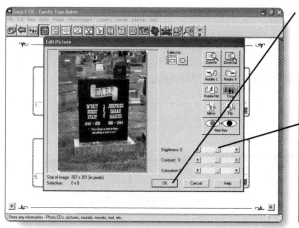

4. Click on **OK**. The changes will be made to the image and the Edit Picture dialog box will close.

TIP

To make dramatic changes to the brightness, contrast, or saturation, use the scroll bar that is located between the buttons for each. You drag to the right to increase or to the left to decrease.

Correcting Red Eye

There are times when the eyes in the pictures of our family look red or hollow. This has long been a frustration of color photos and is now fixable using the scanned images in your scrapbook. Be sure you have opened one of the pictures you want to change.

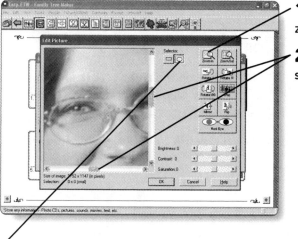

1. Click on the **Zoom In**. The view will zoom in on part of the image.

2. Slide the **scroll bars** until the picture shows the eyes in the image view.

3. Click on the **oval button**. The oval button will be selected.

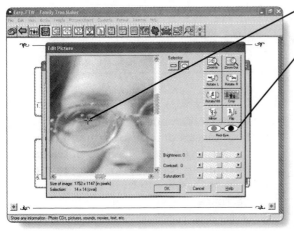

4. Select the **area of the eye** by **dragging the mouse**. The area will be selected.

5. **Click** on the **Red-Eye button**. The Red Eye Removal dialog box will open.

TIP

Generally you will not need to do anything at this point other than to click the OK push button. The red eye removal is automatic. If you do not like it, you can manually adjust the colors.

6a. **Click** on the **right** or **left Red button**. The red in the selected section will be adjusted.

OR

6b. **Click** on the **right** or **left Green button**. The green in the selected section will be adjusted.

OR

6c. **Click** on the **right** or **left Blue button**. The blue in the selected section will be adjusted.

7. **Click** on **OK**. The Red Eye Removal dialog box will close and the picture will reflect the changes made.

NOTE

Be sure to examine the changes to the image by using the Zoom Out to view the picture in its entirety. If you do not like the changes, simply click the Cancel button to close the Edit Picture dialog box and then begin again.

TIP

Family Tree Maker understands that you may use the same photo in more than one scrapbook. When you make changes to an image found in more than one scrapbook, Family Tree Maker will ask you if you want to make changes to just that one scrapbook or to the photo in every scrapbook in which it is found.

Searching for Objects

While it may not seem possible now, the more items you add, the quicker you will need to rely on the abilities of the Find features to locate specific scrapbook objects.

1. **Click** on **Edit**. The Edit menu will appear.

2. **Click** on **Find Picture/Object**. The Find Picture/Object dialog box will open.

NOTE

You must have the scrapbook open to use the Find Picture/Object menu command.

3. **Click** on the **Search down arrow**. The Search drop-down menu will appear.

4. **Click** on the **search option** you want to use. The option will be selected.

5. In the for field, **type** the **term** for which you want to search.

6. **Click** on the **Find next button**. The Family Page window will appear.

7. **Click** on the **Scrapbk button** for the individual who is in the Family Page. The individual's scrapbook will appear, and you will be able to view the scrapbook objects, one of which will fit your search criteria.

NOTE

Continue to click on the Find next button until Family Tree Maker has found the individual you want. Once that person's Family Page is displayed, you can click on the Cancel button to close the Find Individual dialog box.

TIP

Family Tree Maker treats each person's scrapbook separately. You may see a message saying that Family Tree Maker has reached the end of the scrapbook and asking if you want to continue searching. Answering yes will begin the search in other people's scrapbooks.

Sharing Your Scrapbook

When you have put together the digitized images with, say, the digitized interview of your relative, you will want to share it with others.

Playing a Scrapbook

Family reunions are a great place to share scrapbooks. If you have Family Tree Maker set up on a computer with speakers, there is no limit to what you can do.

1. Click on **Picture/Object**. The Picture/Object menu will appear.

2. Click on **Play Scrapbook**. The Play Scrapbook dialog box will open.

3. Use the **up and down arrows** in the Time between Pictures/Objects (in seconds) field to adjust the delay between objects.

4. Click on **OK**. The scrapbook will be played.

TIP

A sound file cannot play at the same time a slide is being viewed. If you have combined the two, you will find that you have a blank screen while the sound file runs its course.

Printing a Scrapbook

Most of the time, you will share your scrapbook by printing it out. Remember, the printed scrapbook includes only digitized still images, such as photographs or documents.

1. **Click** on **File**. The File menu will appear.

2. **Click** on **Print Preview**. The Scrapbook Print Preview window will open.

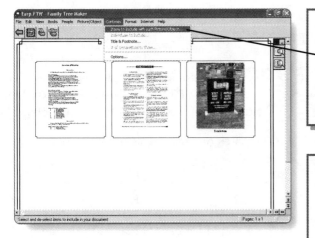

TIP

You can determine what prints in your scrapbook. Click on Contents, and then click on Items to Include with each Picture/Object.

NOTE

You can select box, line and border options on the scrapbook just as you can for many of the other trees and reports. In the Print Preview, click on the Format menu and select Box, Line & Border styles. These options work much the same as those discussed in Chapter 13, "Looking at the Tree Reports in Family Tree Maker."

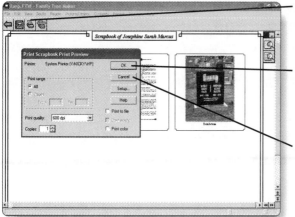

3. **Click** on the **Print button**. The Print Scrapbook Print Preview dialog box will open.

4a. **Click** on **OK**. The scrapbook will be printed.

OR

4b. **Click** on **Cancel**. The scrapbook will not be printed.

TIP

If you want to share the scrapbook through e-mail or upload it to the Internet, instead of printing it, you can export the scrapbook to a PDF file. This is done by clicking on the File menu and selecting Export to PDF, while in the Print Preview view.

18

Creating a Family History Book

For many researchers, the ultimate goal is to publish a record of their ancestry. Family Tree Maker has long kept this in mind and offers one of the easiest ways to put a variety of reports together to share with family, friends, or colleagues. In this chapter, you'll learn how to:

- Select specific reports and trees
- Organize the selected items
- Work with images
- Add page breaks
- Create a customized index

Selecting Available Items

You have looked at many of the trees and reports that Family Tree Maker can create, but you might have been unaware that you can select these and put them together to create a book. One of the first things you have to do is decide what items to select. Following is a list of possible items to include in the book, from the title page to the index, including lots of family trees and narrative reports.

- Front Matter (title page, copyright notice, and so on)
- Introduction
- Ancestor Trees
- Descendant Trees
- Hourglass Trees
- Kinship Reports
- Narrative Reports
- Timelines
- Calendars
- Bibliography
- Index

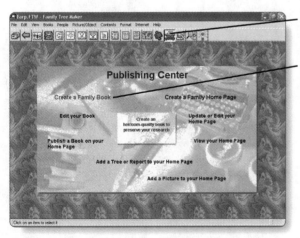

1. **Click** on the **Publishing Center button**. The Publishing Center will appear.

2. **Click** on **Create a Family Book**. The New Book dialog box will open.

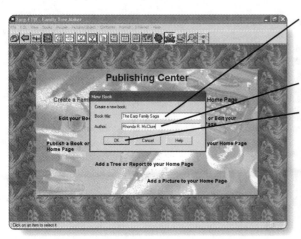

3. **Type** the **book title** in the Book title field and **press** the **Tab key**. The cursor will move to the Author field.

4. **Type** the **author's name**.

5. **Click** on **OK**. The Books window will appear.

TIP

Another way to begin putting together a new book is to click on the Books menu. After the Books menu appears, click on New Book.

Selecting Front Matter

When you open any book, the first pages you look at contain what Family Tree Maker refers to as the front matter. The title page, copyright notice, dedication, and table of contents are such items. When you first create your book, you will need to decide which of these you want to include.

NOTE

When the Books window appears, there is only one item already included in the Outline for list. The Title Page was created when you filled in the information in the New Book dialog box.

---

1. In the Available items list, **double-click** on **Text Item**. The Add text item dialog box will open.

2. **Click** on the desired **text item**. The item will be selected.

3. **Click** on **OK**. The selected text item will be added to the Outline for list.

4. In the Outline for list, **click** on the newly added **text item**. The option buttons will be activated.

5. **Click** on **Edit**. The text editor window will open and display the selected item.

6. **Use** the **toolbar buttons** to make changes to the item.

TIP

The text editor works much like any other word-processing program. If you click on one of the toolbar buttons, such as italics, before you type, then the text will be in italics. To change something that has already been written, you must highlight the text before choosing one of the toolbar options.

7. **Click** on the **Close button**. You will be prompted to save the book item; click on OK.

NOTE

You are not limited to a single text item. You might want to repeat steps 1 through 6 to add additional items such as a copyright notice, a dedication, and an introduction.

Adding Trees and Reports

A book of your ancestors should contain a number of different trees and reports. It is important to keep your audience in mind when you're deciding what to include. You can create different books for different groups of individuals, so that the one you share with your family is more personal and less formal than the one you share with another genealogist.

1. **Click** on the **tree or report** you want to include. The tree or report will be highlighted.

2. **Click** on **Add**. The tree or report will be added to the Outline for list.

TIP

You can select any of the reports, trees, or other options in the Available items list. You will learn to organize them later in this chapter, in the "Organizing the Items" section.

3. **Double-click** on **Genealogy Report**. The Add Genealogy Report dialog box will open.

4. **Select** the **type of Genealogy Report** to add. The option will be selected.

5. **Click** on **OK**. The Add Genealogy Report dialog box will close and the Genealogy Report will appear in the Outline for list.

Including Text with Pictures

Most of your family will want to see pictures in the book you share with them. While you can include them in some of the trees and reports, there are other times when you might want to have more control over the image. You can take this control by adding a Text Item with Pictures.

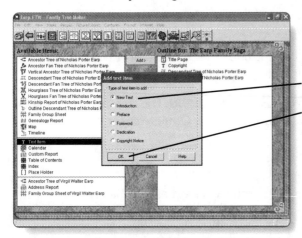

1. In the Available Items list, **double-click** on **Text Item**. The Add text item dialog box will open.

2. **Select** the desired **text item**.

3. **Click** on **OK**. The Add text item dialog box will close.

4. In the Outline for list, **click** on the newly added **text item**. Additional option buttons will be activated.

5. **Click** on **Edit**. The Text Item edit window will open.

6. Click on **Picture**. The Picture menu will appear.

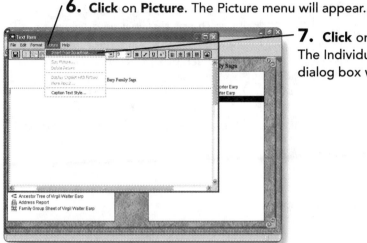

7. Click on **Insert from Scrapbook**. The Individuals with Scrapbook Pictures dialog box will open.

8. Click on the **individual** whose scrapbook you want to access. The individual will be highlighted.

9. Click on **OK**. The Insert Scrapbook Picture dialog box will open.

NOTE

If the displayed individual's scrapbook does not include the picture you were expecting, you can click on Select new individual and the Individuals with Scrapbook Pictures dialog box will open again.

10. **Click** on the **picture** you want to include. The picture will be displayed in the Preview box, if you have the Preview Picture check box selected.

11. **Click** on **OK**. The Insert Scrapbook Picture dialog box will close and the picture will be included in the Text Item window.

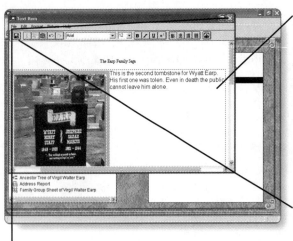

12. **Type** the **text** you want to associate with the image.

TIP

The Text Item window is similar to a word-processing program. You can alter the font and format of the text and the image within that window.

---

13. **Click** on the **Save button**. The changes to the text item will be saved.

14. **Click** on the **Close button**. The Text Item window will close.

Working with Outline Items

After you have decided which reports and trees you want to include in your book, you can begin to organize their order in the Outline for list. This is the order in which they will print when you send your book to the printer. You can also control which of your reports will start a new chapter in the book.

Organizing the Items

When you added to the Outline for list, Family Tree Maker simply placed the newly added tree or report at the bottom of the list. However, this might not be the order in which you want them to print. You can add them in the order you want them to appear, or you can simply move them around after they are in the list.

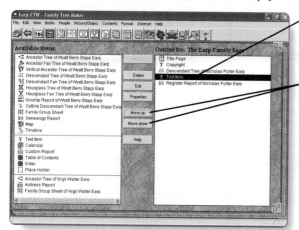

1. In the Outline for list, **click** on the **item** you want to move. The item will be highlighted.

2. Click on the **Move up or Move down button** to move the highlighted item.

NOTE

Although Family Tree Maker doesn't disable the buttons, you cannot move the Title Page. Family Tree Maker will tell you that the Title Page must be the first item in the book.

TIP

It is a good idea to have a plan before you start moving around the reports. For more information about publishing your family history with Family Tree Maker, and for some ideas about different types of family history book projects, you might want to read *Create Your Family History Book with Family Tree Maker Version 8: The Official Guide* (Prima Tech, 2000) by Martha Arends.

Working with Item Properties

As you were putting your reports and trees into the order in which they now appear, you were probably visualizing the divisions of your book. If you look at any of the published family histories in your local genealogy library, you will see that they are broken into chapters to make using the book easier.

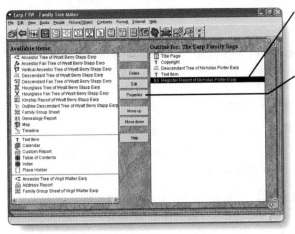

1. **Click** on the **report or tree** with which you want to work. The report or tree will be highlighted.

2. **Click** on the **Properties button**. The Item Properties dialog box will open.

3. **Select** the **This item begins a Chapter check box** if you want the item to be the first item in a new chapter. A check mark will appear in the check box.

4. **Select** the **Start this item on odd numbered page check box** if you want to control on what page this item will begin. A check mark will appear in the check box.

TIP

You can use the Header/Footer options to determine which of your reports and trees will include the header or footer information. The header is usually the title of the book. The footer is usually the page number.

5. **Click** on **OK**. Your changes will be saved and the Item Properties dialog box will close.

Finalizing the Book

Family Tree Maker offers a few enhancements to help to define your book and make it easier to read. After all, you want those who read the book to find it easy to use.

Adding Page Breaks

There might be times when you're working with one of the text items that you want to break up the text or put your images on separate pages. To do this, you will need to add a page break.

1. **Click** on the **text item** you want to edit. The text item will be highlighted.

2. **Click** on the **Edit button**. The Text Item window will appear.

3. **Click** on **Edit**. The Edit menu will appear.

4. **Click** on **Insert Page Break**. A new page will be added in the Text Item window.

TIP

You can undo the page break by putting the insertion point at the top of the page and pressing the Backspace key.

---

5. **Click** on the **Close button**. Family Tree Maker will prompt you to save the changes and the Text Item window will close.

Creating a Customized Index

Family Tree Maker allows you to include an index in your family history book. Genealogists for years to come will be pleased to find that your book has an index. While Family Tree Maker does the hard work of organizing the page numbers, you control the look and feel of the index.

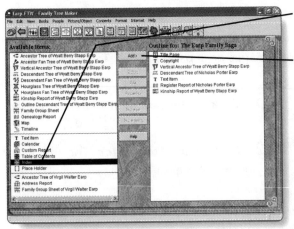

1. **Click** on **Index** in the Available items list. The option will be highlighted.

2. **Click** on **Add**. The index will be added to the end of the Outline for list.

3. In the Outline for list, **click** on **Index**. The option will be highlighted.

4. **Click** on **Edit**. The Index of Individuals Report will appear.

5. **Click** on **Contents**. The Contents menu will appear.

6. **Click** on **Options**. The Options for Book Index dialog box will open.

7. **Click** on the **Columns radio button** to select the number of columns to include in the index. The option will be selected.

8. **Click** on the **Group first names under each surname check box**. A check mark will appear.

9. **Click** on the **Display index letters check box**. A check mark will appear.

10. **Click** on **OK**. Family Tree Maker will make the requested changes to the report.

TIP

You might want to view the index with all possible combinations of these choices to examine the effect each combination has on the ease of reading the index.

19

Creating Your Personal Family Tree Maker Home Page

While publishing a family history is still traditionally done by putting it on paper, the Internet has brought about a marvelous new way for people to publish their family histories. When publishing to paper, people tend to hold off publishing in an effort to get everything perfect. The Internet saves people from this need to delay, as they can always upload a revised version of their pages. In this chapter, you'll learn how to:

- Create your first home page
- Register your home page
- Add reports to your home page
- Add trees to your home page
- Remove items from your home page

Creating Your First Home Page

Computers can intimidate genealogists, and many genealogists consider the Internet to be the biggest computer of them all. Fortunately Family Tree Maker has a wizard that makes creating your first family history Web page on Genealogy.com an easy and enjoyable experience.

Working with the Wizard

Family Tree Maker is following the lead of many other software programs by adding wizards that help you perform certain tasks. The Family Home Page wizard walks you through putting together a basic home page that will be displayed at Genealogy.com.

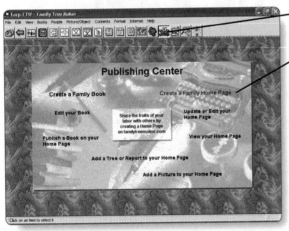

1. **Click** on the **Publishing Center button**. The Publishing Center will appear.

2. **Click** on **Create a Family Home Page**. The Family Home Page wizard will appear.

NOTE

The Family Home Page wizard helps you learn how to create a family history home page on the Genealogy.com Web site.

3. **Click** on the **Next button**. The wizard will begin to ask you questions.

4. Select between **Everyone in your file** and **Selected Individuals only?** The radio button will move to your desired selection.

NOTE

If you have elected to use Selected Individuals only, you will need to use the Select Individuals to Include push button to make your choices. This is the same as the Select Individuals dialog box found in "Choosing Individuals to Include in Your Report" in Chapter 14, "Working with Specialty Reports and the Research Journal."

5. Click on **Next**. The wizard will ask the next question. Continue to answer the questions of the wizard.

TIP

One of the wizard questions asks about hiding the information on living individuals. It is a good idea to select the Hide Info on Living Individuals option. Many people are nervous about identity theft in today's high tech world. Omitting information about living individuals from your Web site helps to protect them from such identity theft and other invasions of privacy.

6. Make sure you are **connected to the Internet** and then **click** on **Next**. The Uploading Homepage status bar will appear.

TIP

The Status bar lets you know how much of your page has already been uploaded. When it has finished uploading you will get a message box telling you of the success of the upload and that the information will be on the Internet within 15 minutes. Click OK to close the message box.

---

7. Click on **Next**. Family Tree Maker will launch your Web browser and the Create Your Own Web Page will open.

Selecting a Theme for Your Home Page

The wizard has put together a general page for you to upload. Once the initial information has been collected and uploaded by Family Tree Maker, you will find that the Create Your Own Home Page will get some specifics about you and how you want the Web site to look.

1. Type in the **title** that you want to appear on your Web page and then **press** the **Tab key**. The cursor will move to the first field of the Contact Information section.

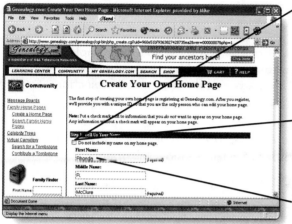

2a. **Click** on the **Do not include my name on my home page box**. The check mark will appear and your name will not be included on the Web page.

OR

2b. **Leave** the **Do not include my name on my home page box** empty and **press the Tab** key to move to the name section of the Contact information.

3. **Type** in **your name** in the three name fields, **pressing** the **Tab** key to move from one field to the next. The cursor will move to the Middle Name field.

TIP

Because this is being posted to the Internet, it is often a good idea to elect not to include your address or phone number on the site. Be sure though to include your e-mail address so that those who come upon your information can get in contact with you. You never know when a cousin will have information to share.

---

4. **Continue** to **supply** information in the Contact Information section.

5. **Type** in the **text** in the Text box and then **press** the **Tab** key. The cursor will move to the Style section.

NOTE

The Text section is where you will want to include information about your research and your purpose for doing the research. It is the introduction that visitors to your site will read, so it is their first impression of you and what you are doing with your research.

---

6. **Choose** a **Style** for your Web page. The radio button will move to that style.

TIP

If you click on the Sample link your browser will show you an example of that style theme. Simply use your Back button in your browser software to return to the Create Your Own Home Page page and finish your style selection.

7. Click on the **Create Home Page Now button**. The page will be created and shown in your browser and the Personal Mail List window will open.

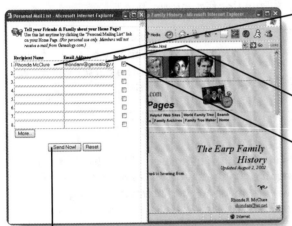

8. Type in the **Recipient's name** in the Recipient Name field and **press** the **Tab** key. The cursor will move to the Email Address field.

9. Type in the **E-mail address** for the recipient in the E-mail Address field.

10. Click on the **Include check box**. The individual will be included in the e-mail message sent alerting them to your new Web page.

TIP

The Personal Mail List is a great way to share with cousins when your combined work is ready for display. You can include more than eight individuals in the mail list and you do not need to worry about Genealogy.com sending them any advertising. This list is for your personal use.

11. Click on the **Send Now button**. A message box will appear telling you that the message has been sent.

Working with Your Home Page

After the wizard has helped you upload that first Web page, you can enhance it by adding additional reports, an InterneTree, or even a book. The beauty of your home page is that you can change what is available whenever you wish. Most of the reports that you can print to paper can be used on the Family Tree Maker site as well.

Adding Reports

Adding reports to your family home page will make them viewable to anyone who visits your Web page. These pages will be added to the indexing and searching functions found on Family Tree Maker's Web site and to the Genealogy.com search page. There are many reports and trees that you can publish to your family home page, including

- Outline Descendant Trees

- Custom Reports

- Genealogy Reports (Register, NGSQ, or Ahnentafel)

- Family Tree Maker Book

1. Click on the **report button** for the tree or report you want to add to your home page. The report will appear.

2. Click on **Internet**. The Internet menu will appear.

3. Click on **Publish Report to the Internet**. The Add a Tree or Report to Your Home Page wizard will open.

TIP

Some trees, such as the Standard Ancestor Tree, will prompt Family Tree Maker to upload an InterneTree, a PDF version of the ancestor tree chart, or both. The PDF version looks like the printed tree, whereas the InterneTree is an interactive pedigree that visitors can navigate through when looking at your research online.

---

4. **Answer** the **question** asked. The wizard will record the answer.

5. **Click** on **Next**. The wizard will ask the next question.

6. **Continue to answer** the wizard's **questions**. When it has asked all the questions, the last page of the wizard will have a Finish button that, once clicked, will upload the report to your Web space at Genealogy.com.

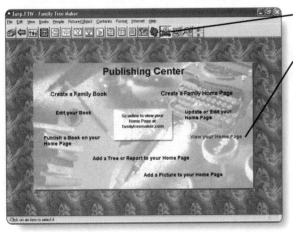

7. **Click** on the **Publishing Center button**. The Publishing Center will appear.

8. **Click** on **View your Home Page**. Your browser will appear.

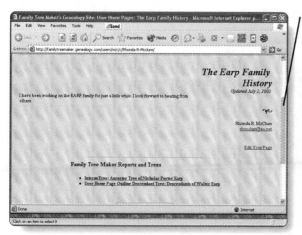

9. Use the **scroll bar** to scan through your Web page.

NOTE

You will see that in addition to working in the Family Tree Maker program, you can also upload other items to your home page, including pictures and Web links. Click on the Add to or Edit This Section link to customize your home page.

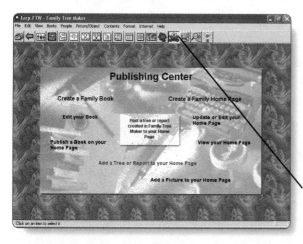

Adding an InterneTree

An InterneTree is a box-style tree. However, unlike the normal box-style reports, this one is interactive. Visitors to your home page can use an index and move through the generations. For each person in the tree, they will see the name, birth date, and death date for the individual.

1. Click on the **Publishing Center button**. The Publishing Center will appear.

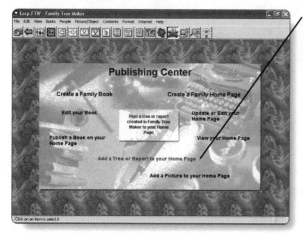

2. Click on **Add a Tree or Report to your Home Page**. The Add a Tree or Report to your Home Page wizard will open.

3. Select an appropriate **tree report**. The report will be selected.

4. Click on the **Next button**. The Select Type of Tree options will appear.

NOTE

If you wish to share your entire database in the InterneTree, the best tree report to select would be the All-in-One tree.

NOTE

You can have only one InterneTree on your site at a time. If you would like other tree reports to be available as well, you will need to select the Graphical Tree option when uploading them.

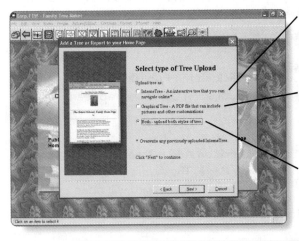

5a. Select the **InterneTree**. The radio button will move to the InterneTree.

OR

5b. Select the **Graphical Tree**. The radio button will move to the Graphical Tree.

OR

5c. Select the **Both** option. The radio button will move to the Both option.

TIP

At the present time, an InterneTree can have as many as 2,000 individuals in it. This is important to remember if you have chosen to upload a report that includes all the individuals in your database.

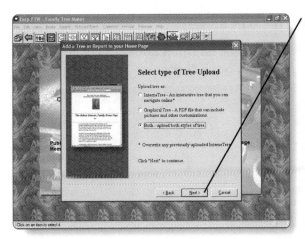

6. Continue to **click Next** as you work through the remainder of the wizard.

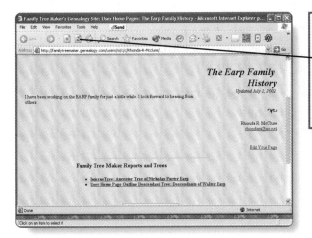

NOTE

You might need to click on the Refresh button in your browser to see the InterneTree in the list of reports on your home page.

Adding a Book

Just as you can print your family history book to paper and publish it to send to your family and fellow researchers, you can also include it on your home page. This offers you the chance to publish your book while it's still a work in progress. As you find new information or correct inaccurate conclusions, you can simply upload a new version of the book to your home page.

1. Click on **Books**. The Books menu will appear.

2. Click on **Open Book**. The Open Book dialog box will open.

3. Select the **book** you want from the Available books list. The book will be highlighted.

4. Click on **OK**. The Book window will appear.

5. Click on **Internet**. The Internet menu will appear.

6. Click on **Publish Book to the Internet**. Family Tree Maker will upload the book, as it has already been designed, to your home page.

> **NOTE**
>
> During this process you will be prompted to add a Table of Contents if your book did not have one yet. You will also be asked if you want to contribute to the World Family Tree. Click Yes if you do or No if you do not. World Family Tree is a compilation of GEDCOM submissions by researchers interested in sharing their information on the *World Family Tree* CD-ROMs.

Removing Items from Your Home Page

Don't think that just because your Family Tree Maker program has uploaded these pages, you have no control over whether they remain on the home page. You determine what stays.

Removing a Family Tree Maker Report or Book

Removing a report or book that you have placed on your home page is not done through the Family Tree Maker program. This is done at the Genealogy.com Web site—specifically, at your home page.

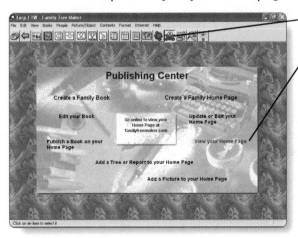

1. **Click** on the **Publishing Button**. The Publishing Center will open.

2. **Click** on **View your Home Page**. Your browser will open and you will be taken to your home page.

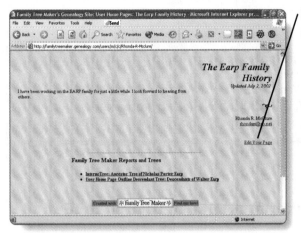

3. Click on **Edit Your Page**. The Author Options page will open in your browser.

4. Scroll to the **Remove Information section** at the bottom of the edit page and **click** on the **link** for the information you want to remove. The Removing page will appear.

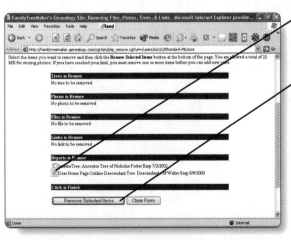

5. Click on the **check box** next to the item you wish to remove. A check mark will appear.

6. Click on the **Remove Selected Items button**. The item(s) will be removed.

Deleting Your Home Page

You are not limited to removing specific items from your home page. You can also delete the entire home page if you need to—you can always re-create it at a later date.

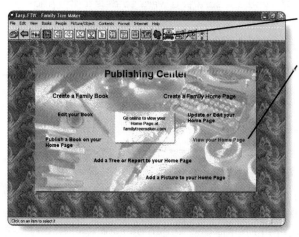

1. Click on the **Publishing Center button**. The Publishing Center will appear.

2. Click on **View Your Home Page**. Your browser will open and take you to your home page.

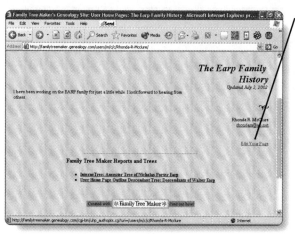

3. Click on **Edit Your Page**. The Author Options Web page will appear.

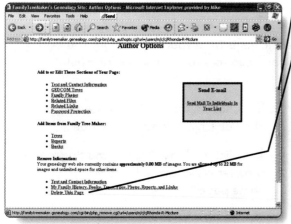

4. **Scroll** down to the **Remove Information section.**

5. **Click** on **Delete This Page**. You will be taken to a page that prompts you again if you are sure you want to delete the page, with push buttons to Delete Home Page and Keep Home Page.

CAUTION

If you elect to delete your home page, all the reports and trees that were available on your home page will no longer show up online. If you do not want to permanently delete your entire home page, then be sure to click on the Keep Home Page button.

Part V Review Questions

1. In Family Tree Maker, what is a scrapbook? *See "Using the Scrapbook" in Chapter 17*

2. What are the three different types of objects you can include in the scrapbook? *See "Inserting Scrapbook Objects" in Chapter 17*

3. How can you rearrange the order of your scrapbook objects? *See "Rearranging Scrapbook Objects" in Chapter 17*

4. What reports can you include in a family history book with Family Tree Maker? *See "Selecting Available Items" in Chapter 18*

5. How can you add a tree or report to your family history book? *See "Adding Trees and Reports" in Chapter 18*

6. How do you include pictures in your family history book? *See "Including Text with Pictures" in Chapter 18*

7. What are the ways you can customize the index to your family history book? *See "Creating a Customized Index" in Chapter 18*

8. What types of reports can you include on your family history home page? *See "Working with Your Home Page" in Chapter 19*

9. How can you add a family history book to your home page? *See "Adding a Book" in Chapter 19*

10. How can you remove a report or book from your home page? *See "Removing a Family Tree Maker Report or Book" in Chapter 19*

PART VI

Advanced Family Tree Maker Methods

20

Working with Dates and Facts

Working with the Marriage field in the Family Page might overshadow some of the other features you have used in the More About Marriage Facts window. Custom facts offer you an unlimited number of life events, though as your experience with the program grows, you might want to do away with some of the facts you have created. In this chapter, you'll learn how to:

- Work with the marriage fact

- Coordinate the Marriage Fact and More About Marriage Facts options

- Remove a previously created custom fact name

- Work with the date calculator to estimate dates

Working with the Marriage Fact

It is almost second nature, as a genealogist, to want to enter a date of marriage for the parents of a family. Understanding how Family Tree Maker works with the information submitted here will prevent frustration when you are generating reports.

It is extremely tempting to fill in a date in the Marriage date field on the Family Page, even when you don't have one. The Marriage date field should be reserved for those times when you have an actual marriage date; for instance, when you have in your possession (or when you have seen) a marriage license or certificate.

Understanding Beginning Status

The Beginning status field can be ignored if you wish. If you are not entering information into the Marriage date field, the Beginning status field might prove useful in helping you to remember what you know about that couple's relationship.

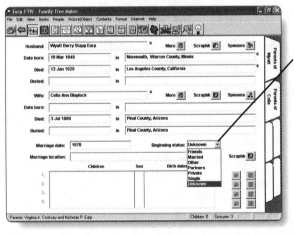

1. Click on the **Family Page Button**. The Family Page will appear.

2. Click on the **Beginning status down arrow**. The Beginning status drop-down list will appear.

TIP

If you hold the mouse pointer over the Beginning status field, a pop-up Help message will appear, explaining the purpose of this option in Family Tree Maker.

3. Click on the **appropriate status**.
The status will be selected.

NOTE

Notice how the wording for the Marriage date and place have changed based on the new Beginning status option. In some reports, this will change the wording of the reports from "married" to "met." On the Family Page, you will see that the word "marriage" has now been changed to "meeting."

Getting Family Page and More About Marriage Facts to Work Together

You will want to pay close attention to the options in the Beginning status menu. When selecting from the More About Marriage Facts menu, you will need to select a preferred marriage fact.

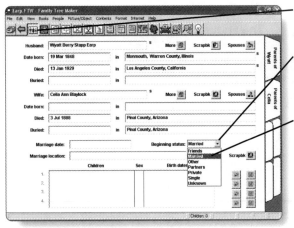

1. **Click** on the **Family Page button**. The Family Page will appear.

2. **Click** on the **Beginning status down arrow**. The Beginning status drop-down menu will appear.

3. **Select** the **Married** status from the list. The option will be selected.

NOTE

Be sure that the Marriage date and Marriage location fields are empty on the Family Page.

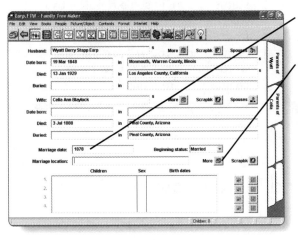

4. **Type** the **marriage date and place**. Make note of the date and location.

5. **Click** on the **More button**. The More About Marriage window will appear.

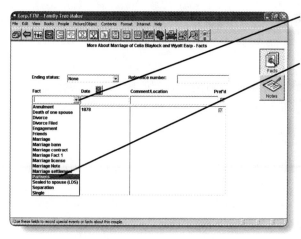

6. **Click** on the **Fact down arrow**. The Fact drop-down menu will appear.

7. **Click** on **Partners**. The Partners fact will be selected.

8. **Press** the **Tab key**. The cursor will move to the Date field.

9. **Type** the **date** and **press** the **Tab key**. The cursor will move to Comment/Location field.

TIP

Be sure that the date in question is different than the marriage date entered earlier.

10. **Type** the **place or comment** and **press** the **Tab key**. The cursor will disappear.

11. **Click** on the **Pref'd check box**. A check mark will appear.

12. **Press** the **Tab key**. The new marriage fact will be placed in the event list.

13. **Click** on the **Family Page button**.

The Family Page will open. Notice that the Family Page has changed. The Marriage date and location fields have been renamed to Meeting date and Meeting location. The date information reflects the new date entered. Also, notice that the Beginning status reflects the Partners selection.

Removing a Custom Fact Name

One of the questions Family Tree Maker users often ask pertains to custom facts that they create and then want to delete.

Verifying No One Is Using the Fact

Before you can do anything with the custom fact name in your Fact list, you must first verify that no one in the database is still linked to the fact.

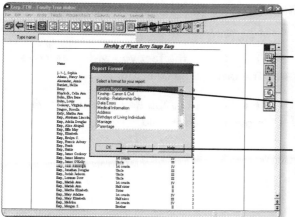

1. Click on the **Report button**. The Report window will open.

2. Click on the **Format button**. The Report Format dialog box will open.

3. Click on **Custom Report**. The Custom Report will be selected.

4. Click on **OK**. The Report Format dialog box will close.

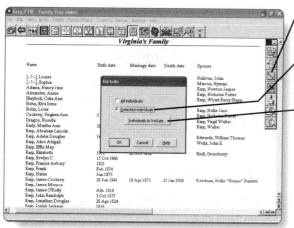

5. Click on the **Individuals to Include button**. The Include dialog box will open.

6. Click on the **Selected individuals radio button**. The option will be selected.

7. Click on the **Individuals to Include button**. The Individuals to Include dialog box will open.

TIP

If there are individuals in the You have included these individuals list, click on the << button to remove them from the list.

8. Click on the **Find> button**. The Add Individuals dialog box will open.

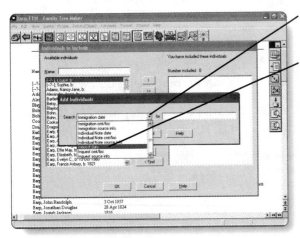

9. **Click** on the **Search down arrow**. The Search drop-down menu will appear.

10. **Select** the **fact** you wish to remove. The fact will be selected.

11. **Press** the **Tab key**. The cursor will move to the for field.

12. **Type !=**.

NOTE

By entering the characters != you are telling Family Tree Maker to show you anyone with anything in that field. This is the best way to find anyone still associated with the fact.

13. **Click** on **OK**. The Add Individuals dialog box will close.

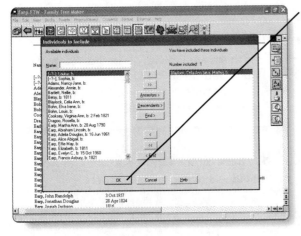

14. **Click** on **OK**. The Individuals to Include dialog box will close.

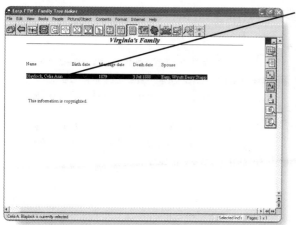

15. **Double-click** on **one of the names** that appear in the report. The Individual Facts Card will open.

16. **Click** on the **fact**. The fact will be highlighted.

17. **Press** the **Delete key.** The fact will be removed from the list of facts for that individual.

18. **Click** on **OK**. The Individual Facts Card will close.

TIP

You will need to repeat steps 15 through 18 for each person who appeared on the Custom Report.

Think Rename, Not Delete

Once you no longer have anyone using the fact, you can get rid of it. You won't actually be deleting the fact; instead, you'll be renaming it. Before beginning this section, be sure to be in the More About Facts window for anyone in your database.

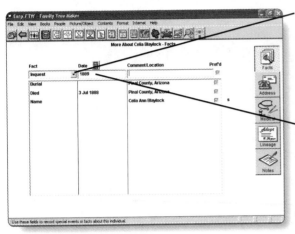

1. Click on the **Fact down arrow**. The Fact drop-down menu will appear.

2. Select the **fact to be removed** and **press** the **Tab key**. The fact will be selected and the cursor will move to the Date field.

3. Type a **date** and **press** the **Tab key** twice. The fact will be added to the More About Facts window.

NOTE

In order for Family Tree Maker to recognize the fact, you must enter either a date or a place. Hitting the Tab key three times will not allow you to add an empty fact to the list. The fact must be added to the list before you can change its name.

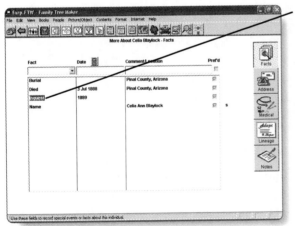

4. Highlight the **name** of the fact to be deleted. That fact name will be selected.

5. Type the **name** of one of the unused facts in the Fact list. The name of the fact will change.

TIP

The Family Tree Maker KnowledgeBase at Genealogy.com suggests changing a fact to be deleted to the Caste event, as this is not often used in your general research.

6. Press the **Tab key**. The Change Fact Name message box will appear.

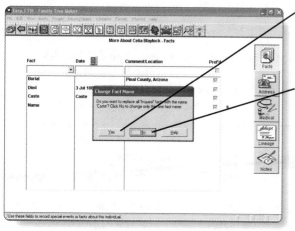

7a. **Click** on **Yes**. The fact name will change for all occurrences of this fact name.

OR

7b. **Click** on **No**. The fact name will not change for all occurrences of this fact name.

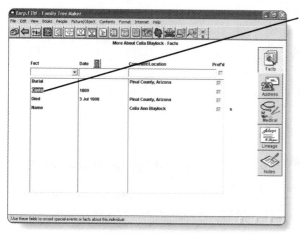

8. **Click** on the **newly named fact**. The fact will be highlighted.

9. **Press** the **Delete key**. The fact name will be deleted.

10. **Press** the **Tab key**. The fact will be removed from the individual's list of facts.

Calculating Dates or Ages

There are times when you discover the age of an individual included in records. Through this information you can calculate the date of birth of the person. At other times you may not know the date of death but you have his age at death. When combined with the date of birth, you can calculate the date of death.

TIP

You have access to the date calculator any time you are in a date field in the Family Page. You will see a similar date calculator icon in the More About Facts page as well as in the Individual Facts Card. You can also access the date calculator by clicking on the People menu and selecting the Date Calculator.

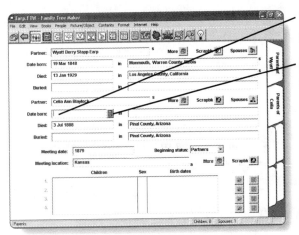

1. **Click** in the **date field** you want to calculate. The date calculator icon will appear.

2. **Click** on the **date calculator**. The Date Calculator dialog box will appear.

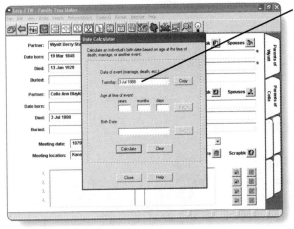

3. **Type** in the **date** of the **known event**.

4. **Press** the **Tab key** twice. The cursor will move to the Age at time of event field.

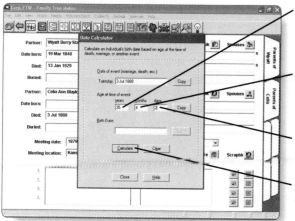

5. Type in the **number of years** in the years field and press Tab. The cursor will move to the months field.

6. Type in the **number of months** in the months field and press Tab. The cursor will move to the days field.

7. Type in the **number of days** in the days field.

8. Click on the **Calculate button**. Family Tree Maker will calculate the date of birth.

NOTE

If you want to calculate the date of death, you would put in the Birth date and the age at time of event field and leave the Date of event field empty. Clicking on the Calculate would then supply you with the date of death.

TIP

To put the birth date in the Birth field of the Family Page, first click on the Copy button then put the cursor in the Birth field of the Family Page and use the CTRL-V hot key to paste the date into the field.

21

Working with GEDCOM Files and Other Family Files

At some point in your research, it is possible that you will get a database from another researcher or you will want to share yours with another. Such sharing is usually done through GEDCOM files. There will also be times when you will want to keep some of your research in a separate Family File. In this chapter, you'll learn how to:

- Export a complete Family File using GEDCOM
- Export a partial Family File using GEDCOM
- Import a GEDCOM file to an existing Family File
- Create a new Family File

Creating a GEDCOM File

When it comes time to share with other researchers, the easiest way to share your information is through a GEDCOM file. This allows researchers to import your work regardless of whether or not they are using Family Tree Maker.

Sharing Your Complete Family File

When sharing with others in your immediate family, you will probably want to share your entire database.

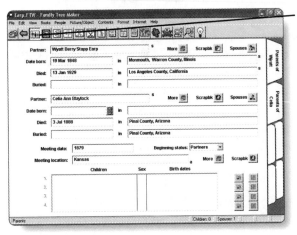

1. **Click** on the **Family Page button**. The Family Page will appear.

2. **Click** on **File**. The File menu will appear.

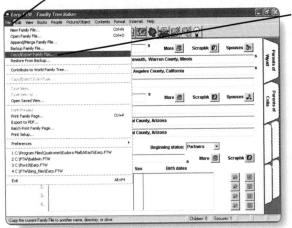

3. **Click** on **Copy/Export Family File**. The New Family File dialog box will open.

NOTE

While Family Tree Maker allows you to add digitized images, sounds, and objects, these links are not supported by GEDCOM. If you share a GEDCOM file, the scrapbook images will not be included in the GEDCOM file.

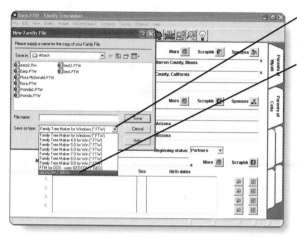

4. **Click** on the **Save as type down arrow**. The Save as type menu will appear.

5. **Click** on **GEDCOM (*.GED)**. The GEDCOM option will be selected.

TIP

Family Tree Maker automatically names the GEDCOM file with the same name you gave the Family File originally. You can double-click on this name to highlight it and type a new name if you want.

NOTE

Pay attention to where Family Tree Maker is saving the file so you can find it later when you want to share it.

---

6. **Click** on the **Save button**. The Export to GEDCOM dialog box will open.

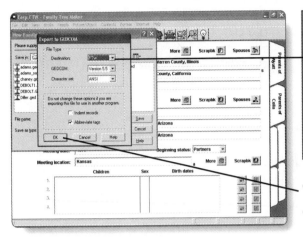

NOTE

Generally the default settings will work when sharing a GEDCOM file. However, if you are a Latter-Day Saint creating a file for TempleReady, you will want to use the Destination drop-down menu to select TempleReady.

7. **Click** on **OK**. The Export to GEDCOM dialog box will close and the file will be saved.

Sharing Part of a Family File

Usually when you are sharing with individuals you have met through a genealogical society or on the Internet, you will only want to send them the line that you share in common.

TIP

To determine the individual to select, first you need to determine the line you want to share. Find the child of that line in the Index of Individuals.

1. **Press** the **F2 key**. The Index of Individuals dialog box will open.

2. **Click** on the **appropriate individual**. He or she will be selected.

3. **Click** on **OK**. The Index of Individuals dialog box will close.

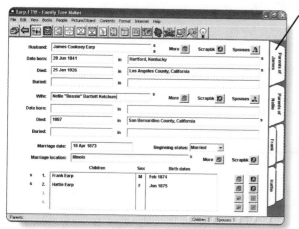

4. Click on the **Parents of tab** for the spouse of the selected individual. The Family Page will display the new family.

NOTE

You must remove the spouse from any parents so that you get only the lineage that you want. If you do not unlink the spouse from his or her parents you in effect get the entire database when you create the GEDCOM file.

5. Click on the **spouse as a child**. The child will be highlighted.

6. Click on **People**. The People menu will appear.

7. Move the **mouse pointer** to Fix Relationship Mistakes. The Fix Relationship Mistakes menu will appear.

8. Click on **Detach Child**. The child will be detached from his or her parents.

NOTE

For a refresher on how to detach a child, see Chapter 12, "Fixing Relationships and Duplicates." In this case, you are temporarily detaching the child. You do not want to detach the siblings.

---

9. **Use** the **Index of Individuals** to relocate the individual selected in step 2.

10. **Click** on the **All-in-One Tree button** on the tool bar. The All-in-One Tree will open.

11. **Click** on the **Options button** on the formatting tool bar along the right side of the screen. The Options for All-in-One Tree dialog box will open.

TIP

While this example is using the All-in-One Tree to isolate the desired individuals, you also can create a list of individuals using the Custom Report. For detailed information on searching for individuals to include in the Custom Report, see Chapter 22, "Working with the Custom Report."

---

12. **Click** on the **Show unconnected step-family trees check box**. The option will be selected.

13. **Click** on **OK**. The Options for All-in-One Tree dialog box will close.

14. **Click** on **File**. The File menu will appear.

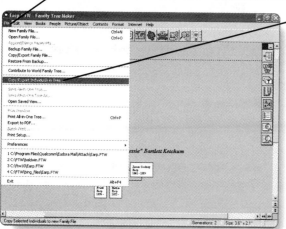

15. **Click** on **Copy/Export Individuals in Tree**. The Copy/Export Individuals in All-in-One Tree dialog box will open.

NOTE

At this point, you can select the GEDCOM option from the Save as type drop-down menu and name the file, as you did earlier in the "Sharing Your Complete Family File" section.

Importing a GEDCOM File into an Existing Family File

Just as you will share GEDCOM files, you will also receive them. You can import a GEDCOM file directly into your Family File. However, this must be done from the Family Page.

TIP

Before beginning this process, it is a good idea to save your Family File as a backup, either by copying it elsewhere on your hard drive or by selecting Backup Family File from the File menu, which is discussed later in this chapter under "Saving a Backup of Your Family File."

1. **Click** on **File**. The File menu will appear.

2. **Click** on **Append/Merge Family File**. The Append Family File dialog box will open.

NOTE

Before you add someone's GEDCOM file to your Family File, it is a good idea to first create a new Family File of the data. This allows you to evaluate the data before it gets mixed in your own Family File. Once you have determined its accuracy, you can then follow the steps in this section to add it to your personal Family File. To see how to create a new Family File with a GEDCOM file, see the "Opening a GEDCOM File as a New Family File" section later in this chapter.

3. **Click** on the **Files of type down arrow**. The Files of Type menu will appear.

4. **Click** on **GEDCOM (*.GED)**. The GEDCOM file type will be selected.

TIP

These same steps can be used to append someone else's Family File or another one you have created. Instead of selecting GEDCOM (*.GED) from the Files of type menu, you would select Family Tree Maker for Windows (*.FTW).

5. **Click** on the **GEDCOM file**. The file will be selected.

6. **Click** on the **Append file button**. A warning message will appear.

7. **Click** on **OK**. The warning message will close and the Import from GEDCOM dialog box will open.

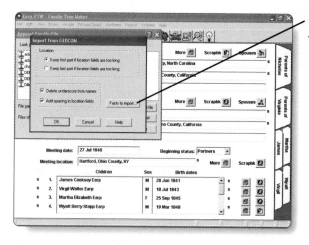

8. **Click** on the **Facts to import button**. The Facts to Import dialog box will open.

NOTE

It is a good idea to look and see where Family Tree Maker wants to put some of the facts that will be imported. This is even more important when the GEDCOM file you are importing is coming from someone who is not using Family Tree Maker.

9. Click on **OK**. The Facts to Import dialog box will close.

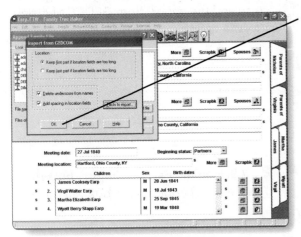

10. Click on **OK**. The Import from GEDCOM dialog box will close, the GEDCOM file will be appended to the Family File, and a message box will open.

11. Click on **OK**. The message box will close and the Individuals to Include dialog box will open.

NOTE

This dialog box is the same as the one you were introduced to in Chapter 10, "Searching Your Family Tree File." Usually you will select everyone in the GEDCOM file using the >> button.

12. Click on **OK**. The Append File dialog box will open.

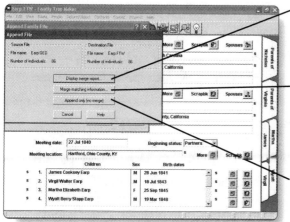

13a. **Click** on **Display merge report**. The Merge Individual Report will open.

OR

13b. **Click** on **Merge matching information**. The Merge Individuals dialog box will open.

OR

13c. **Click** on **Append only (no merge)**. The Append File dialog box will close and the individuals will be added to your database.

TIP

If you need a refresher on how to check the Family File for duplicates, see Chapter 12, "Fixing Relationships and Duplicates."

Opening a GEDCOM File as a New Family File

In addition to appending a GEDCOM file to an existing Family File, you can also create a new Family File using a GEDCOM file as the source of the data.

1. **Click** on **File**. The File menu will appear.

2. **Click** on **Open Family File**. The Open Family File dialog box will open.

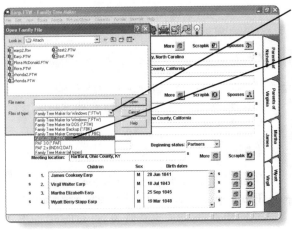

3. **Click** on the **Files of type down arrow**. The Files of type menu will appear.

4. **Click** on **GEDCOM (*.GED)**. The GEDCOM file type will be selected.

NOTE

If you have not saved your Family Files in the default Family Tree Maker directory, you might need to use the Look in drop-down menu to select the appropriate folder on your system where the Family File is stored.

5. **Click** on the **GEDCOM file**. The file will be selected.

6. **Click** on the **Open button**. The New Family File dialog box will open.

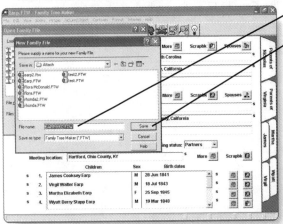

7. **Type** the **name** of the new Family File.

8. **Click** on the **Save button**. The Import from GEDCOM dialog box will open.

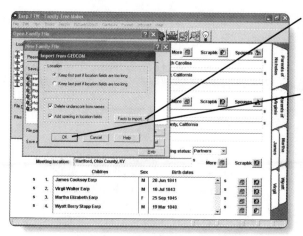

9a. **Click** on the **Facts to import button**. The Facts to Import dialog box will open.

OR

9b. **Click** on **OK**. A message box will appear, telling you the import is complete.

10. If you followed Step 9b, **click** on **OK** to close the message box and go into the new Family File.

Opening a Different Family File

As your research progresses, it is conceivable that you might have more than one Family File. You might decide to create a Family File for a single-surname study or to keep a record of all those individuals to whom you haven't been able to figure out a connection.

Using the Open Family File Option

When you open a Family File, you are actually doing two things. As you tell Family Tree Maker to open the other Family File, Family Tree Maker also closes the currently open Family File.

1. **Click** on **File**. The File menu will appear.

2. **Click** on **Open Family File**. The Open Family File dialog box will open.

TIP

You can also open the Open Family File dialog box by pressing Ctrl+O.

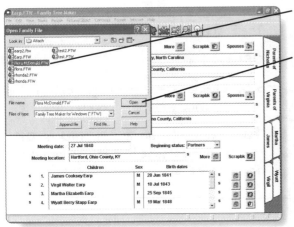

3. **Click** on the **Family File** you want to open. The file will be selected.

4. **Click** on the **Open button**. The Family File will open.

> ### NOTE
>
> The Append file button in the Open Family File dialog box allows you to append another Family File to the last Family File you had open. It works much the same as appending a GEDCOM file, discussed earlier in this chapter.

> ### TIP
>
> There are times when Family Tree Maker will question whether you are a member of the Family File. It might also ask you if you want to run a FamilyFinder report. If you would like to run a FamilyFinder report, click on Yes and Family Tree Maker will run the report from the Internet. For more information, see Chapter 10 "Searching Your Family Tree File."

Using File History

Family Tree Maker will remember the last four Family Files you worked with, including the presently open Family File. You can access this history list to return to a previous Family File.

1. **Click** on **File**. The File menu will appear.

2. **Click** on the **desired Family File**. That Family File will replace the Family File that is currently open.

Saving a Backup of Your Family File

It is a good idea to frequently save a backup of your family file. If you have added a lot of new information or new individuals, that is a perfect time to create a backup so that all your hard work is not lost, should something go wrong.

1. **Click** on **File**. The File menu will appear.

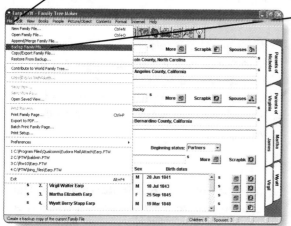

2. **Click** on **Backup Family File**. The Backup Family File dialog box will open.

NOTE

You will need to save the backup file somewhere. It is easiest to save it to your hard drive. However, you should also copy that backup file to another medium (such as a floppy disk, a Zip Disk, a CD-ROM disc, or upload it to the Internet) so that you have it in more than one place should something happen.

3a. **Click** on **Floppy Drive**. The radio button will move to Floppy Drive.

OR

3b. **Click** on **Working Directory**. The radio button will move to Working Directory.

OR

3c. **Click** on **Custom Directory**. The radio button will move to Custom Directory.

NOTE

You can only use the Change filename or directory... push button to select the directory you would like to use or change the name of the file, if you select the Custom Directory.

4. If you have selected the Custom Directory, **click** on **Change filename or directory...** to select the appropriate sub-directory or change the name of the file. The Change filename or directory window will open.

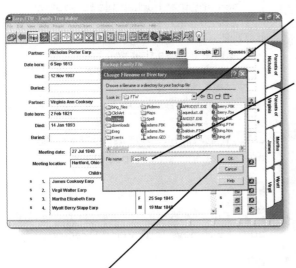

5. Click on the **Look in down arrow**. The Look in directory list will appear where you can select the appropriate sub-directory.

6. Double click in the **File name field**. The file name will be selected.

7. Type in the **file name**. The name of the backup file will change.

TIP

You will not want to change the .FBC extension of the file name. This is a necessary file extension for Family Tree Maker to recognize that the file is a backup file.

8. Click on **OK**. The Change filename or directory window will close.

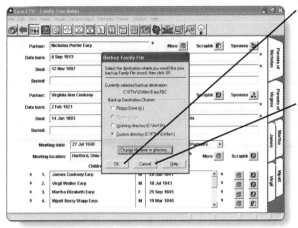

9a. **Click** on **OK**. The Backup family file dialog box will close and Family Tree Maker will save the backup file.

OR

9b. **Click** on **Cancel**. The Backup family file dialog box will close and Family Tree Maker will not save the backup file.

22

Working with the Custom Report

As your research progresses, you will find that the number of individuals in your Family File prevents you from knowing each one personally. The Custom Report allows you to generate a report of selected individuals, geared toward the research you need to do at any given time. In this chapter, you'll learn how to:

- Use Custom Reports to select individuals based on a common name, date, or location
- Use Custom Reports to select individuals based on relationship
- Use find features to remove individuals from a custom report
- Format the custom report
- Save the individuals in the custom report as a new family file

Using the Find Button to Include Individuals in the Custom Report

The Custom Report is a robust tool to use when planning a research trip to a county courthouse or localized regional facility. With the search functions of the Custom Report, you can create a report of just those individuals who fit your research criteria.

1. Click on the **Report button**. The Report window will open.

2. Click on the **Format button**. The Report Format dialog box will open.

3. Click on **Custom Report**. The Custom Report will be selected.

4. Click on **OK**. The Report Format dialog box will close.

Searching by Name

There will be times when your research is in a manuscript collection or other compilation devoted to a given family name. Compiling a list of those individuals in your database helps to guarantee that as you research in these records, you do not overlook anyone presently included in your Family File.

1. Click on the **Individuals to Include button**. The Include dialog box will open.

NOTE

The Custom Report will reveal the list of the last individuals selected. This could be all of the individuals in your Family File or it could be a selected group. The individuals included in the current report are displayed along the bottom of the Family Tree Maker window.

2. Click on the **Individuals to Include button**. The Individuals to Include dialog box will open.

3. Click on the **Find> button**. The Add Individuals dialog box will open.

TIP

Because the report's list of individuals is cumulative, if there is anyone in the You have included these individuals list, you will want to remove them before opening the Add Individuals dialog box. You can remove them by clicking on the << button.

4. Click on the **Search down arrow**. The Search menu will appear.

5. Click on **Name**. The Name search will be selected.

6. Press the **Tab key**. The cursor will move to the for field.

7. Type the **surname** you want to find.

8. Click on **OK**. The You have included these individuals list will change.

9. Click on **OK**. The Custom Report will be modified.

TIP

Because the list of individuals is cumulative, you can repeat steps 3 through 8 to add other surnames to your list. This is useful when you are going to a courthouse in a county where many of the families lived.

Searching by Date

There will be times when the records you are using will be date sensitive. Searching for specific dates in your Family File will include those individuals in the Custom Report, ensuring that you don't overlook anyone.

1. Click on the **Individuals to Include button**. The Include dialog box will open.

2. Click on the **Individuals to Include button**. The Individuals to Include dialog box will open.

3. Click on the **<< button**. Everyone from the You have included these individuals list will be removed.

4. Click on the **Find> button**. The Add Individuals dialog box will open.

5. Click on the **Search down arrow**. The Search menu will appear.

6. Click on the **selected date**. That event date will be selected.

7. Press the **Tab key**. The cursor will move to the for field.

TIP

To create a blanket search of all date fields, select Any and all date fields from the Search menu. This will tell Family Tree Maker to search all fact dates in your Family File.

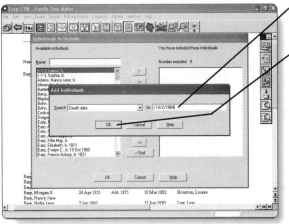

8. Type the **date** for which you want to search.

9. Click on **OK**. The You have included these individuals list will be updated.

Table 22.1 shows you the many ways you can search for dates in your Family File.

Table 22.1

If you type this	Family Tree Maker will find this
<10/2/1998, or BEFORE 10/2/1988, or BEF 10/2/1988	All dates before October 2, 1988, including dates entered as "Before October 2, 1988"
<=10/2/1988	The date October 2, 1988 and all dates before it, including dates entered as "Before October 2, 1988"
>10/2/1988, or AFTER 10/2/1988, or AFT 10/2/1988	All dates after October 2, 1988, including dates entered as "After October 2, 1988"
>=10/2/1988	The date October 2, 1988 and all dates after it, including dates entered as "After October 2, 1988"
ABOUT 10/2/1988, or CIRCA 10/2/1988, or EST 10/2/1988	All dates entered as "About October 2, 1988," "Circa October 2, 1988," or "Est October 2, 1988"
10/2/1988..10/2/1990, or >=10/2/1988..<=10/2/1990	All dates between October 2, 1988 and October 2, 1990, including those two days
>10/2/1988..<10/2/1990	All dates between October 2, 1988 and October 2, 1990, not including those two days
UNKNOWN or ?	All dates entered as "Unknown" or "?"

Searching by Location

When you incorporate the location search in your Custom Report, you create an effective research tool for working in the records. Knowing who was born or married, who died, or who was living in a locality you will be researching ensures that you will have a list of all individuals with you. That way, you will not have to wonder if you overlooked someone.

1. **Click** on the **Individuals to Include button**. The Include dialog box will open.

2. **Click** on the **Individuals to Include button**. The Individuals to Include dialog box will open.

3. **Click** on the **<< button**. Everyone from the You have included these individuals list will be removed.

4. **Click** on the **Find> button**. The Add Individuals dialog box will open.

5. **Click** on the **Search down arrow**. The Search menu will appear.

6. **Click** on the **selected event location**. That event location will be selected.

7. **Press** the **Tab key**. The cursor will move to the for field.

8. Type the **location** for which you want to search.

9. Click on **OK**. The You have included these individuals list will be updated.

TIP

To generate a Custom Report of individuals who were born, married, and died in a given locality, you will need to follow steps 4 through 9 three times, selecting Birth location, Marriage location, and then Death location from the Search drop-down menu.

NOTE

Don't forget to rename the title of your report. For a refresher on this, see Chapter 16, "Creating Genealogy Style and Genealogical Source Reports."

Searching by Relationship

Using the relationship search in the Custom Report is an excellent way to create a report of individuals that can then be saved to a GEDCOM file or a new Family File.

1. Click on the **Individuals to Include button**. The Include dialog box will open.

2. Click on the **Individuals to Include button**. The Individuals to Include dialog box will open.

3. Click on the **<< button**. Everyone from the You have included these individuals list will be removed.

4. Click on the **selected individual** in the Available individuals list. The individual will be selected.

5. Click on the **Find> button**. The Add Individuals dialog box will open.

6. Click on the **Search down arrow**. The Search menu will appear.

7. Click on the **selected relationship**. The relationship will be selected.

8. Click on **OK**. The You have included these individuals list will be updated.

TIP

Two of the available relationship searches can be accomplished using the Ancestors> or Descendants> buttons. If you want to generate a search of descendants of an individual that does not include spouses, you will need to use the option found in the Add Individuals dialog box (accessed by clicking on the Find> button).

NOTE

You can combine any or all of these different searches to come up with the exact group of individuals you want in your Custom Report. First decide what your goal is and then figure out which of the many search options will help you fulfill that goal. Don't get discouraged if you have to try different approaches to the search. You will get it eventually.

Using the Find Button to Remove Individuals

After you have created a list of individuals using the myriad searches available, you might discover that you want to remove selected individuals from the list, especially if you are trying to create a report of individuals from which to generate a new Family File or GEDCOM file.

1. Click on the **individual** in the You have included these individuals list. The individual will be selected.

2. Click on the **<Find button**. The Remove Individuals dialog box will open.

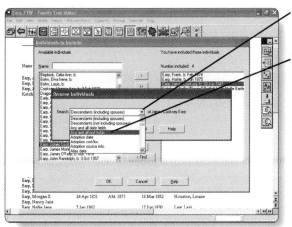

3. **Click** on the **Search down arrow**. The Search menu will appear.

4. **Click** on the desired **search option**. The option will be selected.

> ### NOTE
>
> You have the same search options in the Find and Remove (<Find) search as you had in the Find and Include (Find>) search. It just works in reverse, removing those individuals who fit the search criteria.

5. **Press** the **Tab key**. The cursor will move to the for field.

6. **Type** the **text, date, or name** for which you want to search.

7. **Click** on **OK**. The You have included these individuals list will be updated.

> ### TIP
>
> Once you have the You have included these individuals list to your liking, click on OK in the Individuals to Include dialog box to close it. The Custom Report will then be updated.

Formatting Your Custom Report

Once you have finally selected the individuals for your Custom Report, you will want to take as much care in the design of the report. You want to make sure it has enough information to easily identify the individuals included on the report.

1. **Click** on **Items to Include**. The Items to Include in Report dialog box will open.

2. **Click** on the **<< button**. The Each row of your report will contain list will be erased.

3. **Click** on an **item** in the Available items list. The item will be selected.

4. **Click** on the **Include button**. The Options dialog box will open.

NOTE

For most of the items, the Options dialog box will simply question whether you want to include only preferred dates.

5. **Click** on the **Format down arrow**. The Format menu will appear.

6. **Click** on the **appropriate format**. The format will be selected

NOTE

As you make your choices, the sample in the lower-left corner of the dialog box will change.

7. **Click** on **OK**. The Options dialog box will close and the item will be listed in the Each row of your report will contain list.

TIP

Your report will probably need to contain the name of the individuals, at least one date (for identification purposes), and perhaps the name of the spouse (to make it easier to search for females during your research).

Saving as a New Family File or GEDCOM File

Once you have created the Custom Report that you want, you might want to create a new Family File or GEDCOM file of those individuals.

TIP

Be sure you have your Custom Report open and that it has just the people you want to include in the new file. Only those who appear on the Custom Report will be included in the new file.

1. **Click** on **File**. The File menu will appear.

2. **Click** on **Copy/Export Individuals in Report**. The Copy/Export Individuals in Report dialog box will open.

3. **Type** the **name** of the new file.

4. **Select** the appropriate **option** from the Save as type menu. The Save as type will be chosen.

5. **Click** on the **Save button**.

NOTE

If you are creating a new Family File, Family Tree Maker will begin to export the individuals' information into the file. If you are creating a GEDCOM file, refer to Chapter 21, "Working with GEDCOM Files and Other Family Files" for more information.

23

Working with System Preferences

Family Tree Maker is a powerful program that offers many features and options. Better still, Family Tree Maker allows you, the user, to define your preferences for many of the screens and more common activities. In this chapter, you'll learn how to:

- Establish Fastfields
- Select screen labels for the Family Page
- Protect information on living relatives before sharing data
- Select FamilyFinder preferences
- Work with cue card preferences
- Customize the toolbar buttons
- Learn about the number of individuals in your database

Changing System Preferences

System preferences affect the feel of the program and the way it responds to certain input, and they can be changed or selected so that each time you use the program, you get the same look or response.

Establishing Fastfields

One of the reasons why people use software programs in their genealogy research is to cut down on duplication. One of the ways Family Tree Maker aids in this is through the Fastfields.

1. **Click** on **File**. The File menu will appear.

2. **Move** the **mouse pointer** to **Preferences**. The Preferences menu will appear.

3. **Click** on **Fastfields**. The Fastfields dialog box will open.

TIP

The default setting is to have all of the Fastfields turned on. To turn any of them off, simply click on the check box next to the one that you want to turn off. If there is no check mark in the box, the Fastfield has been turned off.

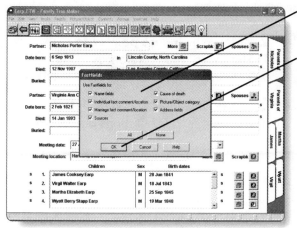

4. Check or uncheck any of the desired **Fastfield options**.

5. Click on **OK**. The changes will be saved and the Fastfields dialog box will close.

NOTE

Fastfields are designed so that you can begin typing the first few letters of a place name, for instance, and Family Tree Maker will supply you with a previously entered place that shares the same first few letters. If it is the place you want, press the Tab key to accept that place and move the cursor. If it isn't the place you want, continue typing the place name.

TIP

If you find that a Fastfield word is misspelled or you want to get rid of it, click on the Trash can next to the word. This will delete it from the Fastfield. You can then type in the correct word.

Selecting Family Page Labels

The default setting for the Family Page and the reports is Husband and Wife. Some people do not like to use these terms, instead preferring something like Father and Mother. Family Tree Maker allows you to make changes to these labels.

1. **Click** on **File**. The File menu will appear.

2. **Move** the **mouse pointer** to **Preferences**. The Preferences menu will appear.

3. **Click** on **Labels and LDS Options**. The Labels and LDS Options dialog box will open.

TIP

You can change one or all of the labels, or you can restore the default labels by clicking on the Reset labels to default button.

4. **Type** the **label name** in the Husband field. This will replace the word Husband on the Family Page and in reports.

5. **Press** the **Tab key**. The cursor will move to the Wife field.

6. **Type** the **label name** in the Wife field. This will replace the word Wife on the Family Page and in reports.

7. **Press** the **Tab key**. The cursor will move to the Marriage field.

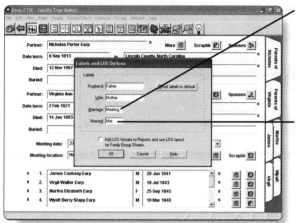

8. **Type** the **label name** in the Marriage field. This will replace the word Marriage on the Family Page and in reports.

9. **Press** the **Tab key**. The cursor will move to the Married field.

10. **Type** the **label name** in the Married field. This will replace the word Married on the reports.

CAUTION

Making these changes will affect your entire Family File.

TIP

If you are a Latter-Day Saint or you prefer that style of Family Group Sheet, you might want to click on the Add LDS formats to Reports and use LDS layout for Family Group Sheets check box. When you do this, you disable the labels, as the LDS format has its own labels.

Protecting Privacy

There has been much concern of late, especially in the genealogical community, about the sharing of information on living individuals. Family Tree Maker allows you to privatize this information.

1. **Click** on **File**. The File menu will appear.

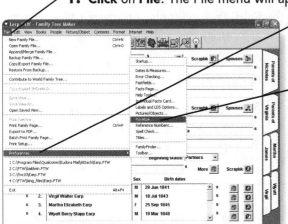

2. **Move** the **mouse pointer** to **Preferences**. The Preferences menu will appear.

3. **Click** on **Privatize**. The Privatize Information dialog box will open.

NOTE

The privatize option is intended as a temporary setting. It is designed to hide the Birth, Death, Marriage, More About Facts, Medical, and Notes information on living relatives so that you can share your database without passing along information on living individuals.

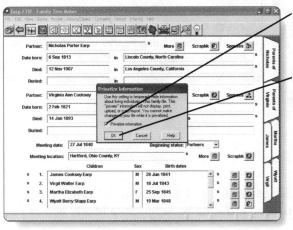

4. **Click** on the **Privatize information check box**. A check mark will appear in the check box.

5. **Click** on **OK**. The Privatize Information dialog box will close.

NOTE

While your Family File is in privatize mode you cannot make any changes to the file. Once you have created the GEDCOM file or printed out the report you want to share, you will need to repeat steps 1 through 5 to turn off the privatize option so that you can make changes to the Family File.

TIP

You will know when your file is in privatize mode because the Family page background will change from yellow to green.

Working with FamilyFinder Preferences

The FamilyFinder Report is a useful tool that lets you know of possible matching information on the Genealogy.com Web site or on the many Family Tree Maker CD-ROMs.

1. Click on **File**. The File menu will appear.

2. Move the **mouse pointer** to **Preferences**. The Preferences menu will appear.

3. Click on **FamilyFinder**. The FamilyFinder dialog box will open.

TIP

The options in the FamilyFinder dialog box are turned on when there is a check mark in the check box. If you prefer not to see the stars on your Family Page, you will need to click on the Show star on Family Page check box to remove the check mark.

NOTE

You can change the number of stars from 1 to 5 when including the stars on the Family Page. It is a good idea to use a higher setting because then you know that when there is a star, the FamilyFinder Report was a high match.

Working with Cue Cards Preferences

The cue cards that pop up as you move from one section of the program to another often include helpful hints and shortcuts so that you get more out of the program. You can turn them on or off as you need.

1. Click on **File**. The File menu will appear.

2. Move the **mouse pointer** to **Preferences**. The Preferences menu will appear.

3. Click on **Help Tools**. The Help Tools dialog box will open.

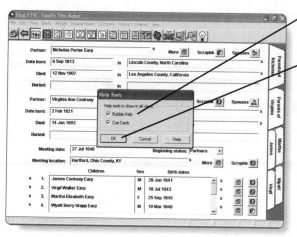

4. **Check or uncheck** either of the **help tools**.

5. **Click** on **OK**. The changes will be saved and the Help Tools dialog box will close.

Customizing the Toolbar

While Family Tree Maker has set up the toolbar with those options that are considered the most popular, it is possible that you might rely more heavily on something not currently available on the toolbar. You can remove buttons, rearrange their order, and add new ones.

1. **Click** on **File**. The File menu will appear.

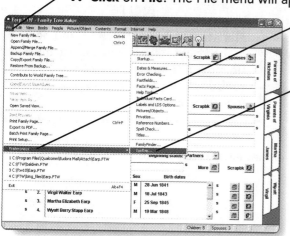

2. **Move** the **mouse pointer** to **Preferences**. The Preferences menu will appear.

3. **Click** on **Toolbar**. The Customize Toolbar dialog box will open.

4. **Click** on an **available item**. The item will be selected.

5. **Click** on the **> button**. The item will be added to the bottom of the Your toolbar Contains list.

6. **Click** on the **newly added item** in the Your toolbar Contains list. The item will be selected.

7. **Click** on the **Move Up button**. The item will move up in the Your toolbar Contains list.

NOTE

The items that you move up and down in the Your toolbar Contains list will be moved to the left or right on the toolbar once you have finished making changes.

8. **Click** on **OK**. The Customize Toolbar dialog box will close and the toolbar will be updated.

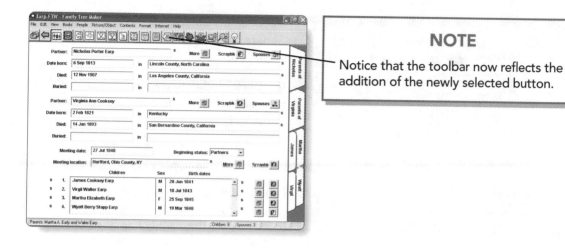

NOTE

Notice that the toolbar now reflects the addition of the newly selected button.

Family File Statistics

Family Tree Maker keeps track of a number of different items in your family file including the number of individuals and the number of marriages. You can also have Family Tree Maker calculate how many surnames there are in the database as well as the total number of generations. Most people just like to know how many people they have in the database.

1. **Click** on **Help**. The Help menu will appear.

2. **Click** on **Family File Statistics**. The Family File Statistics dialog box will open.

3. **Click** on **Calculate**. The number of Generations in the database will be displayed.

4. **Click** on **Calculate**. The number of different Surnames in the database will be displayed.

NOTE

In addition to the number of individuals and marriages in the database, the Family File Statistics dialog box also shows you the average lifespan and the earliest birth date found in the family file.

---

5. **Click** on **Close**. The Family File Statistics dialog box will close.

24

Enhancing Your Family History Book

While the Book feature in Family Tree Maker offers many valuable options for creating a family history book, it is also possible to add additional reports and outside material to your book. In this chapter, you'll learn how to:

- Select additional reports in advance
- Use the Save View As option
- Rename the items in the Outline view
- Add place holders for outside material
- Add additional items to a previously saved book

Preparing Reports in Advance

People often do not think about the reports that they would like to include in their book until they are actually in the Books window. However, you can create specific reports ahead of time and then incorporate them into one or all of your books.

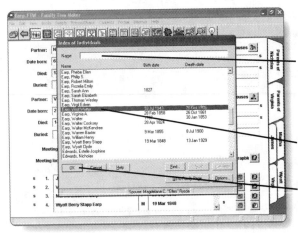

1. **Press** the **F2 key**. The Index of Individuals dialog box will open.

2. **Type** part of the **name** of the individual you want for the report. The highlight bar will move to the first person whose name contains those letters.

3. **Click** on the **individual** you want to select. That person will be highlighted.

4. **Click** on **OK**. The Index of Individuals dialog box will close.

Selecting and Formatting Reports

You must first decide the goal of these additional reports. For instance, do you want a chapter of Family Group Sheets on each family that will be found in the narrative section of the book?

1. **Click** on the **Family Group Sheet button**. The Family Group Sheet for the individual you selected will appear.

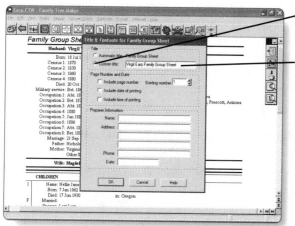

TIP

If you are going to create a chapter of Family Group Sheets in your book, you might want to change the generic "Family Group Sheet" title on each Family Group Sheet Report you generate to better represent who is included in the report.

2. Click on **Contents**. The Contents menu will appear.

3. Click on **Title & Footnote**. The Title & Footnote for Family Group Sheet dialog box will open.

4. Click on the **Custom title radio button**. The cursor will move to the Custom title field.

5. Type the **new title** for the Family Group Sheet.

TIP

You might want to use the name of the father as your title if you will be creating many Family Group Sheets for your book.

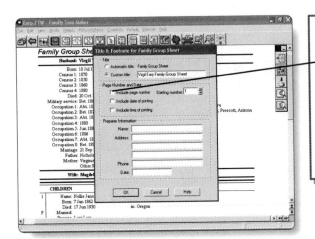

NOTE

Because this Family Group Sheet is going to be part of your overall book, you will want to turn off the Include page number option. The page number will be added and controlled by the placement of the Family Group Sheet in your book.

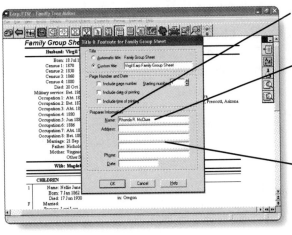

6. **Click** in the **Name field**. The cursor will move to the Name field.

7. **Type** the **name** of the preparer and **press** the **Tab key**. The cursor will move to the first Address field.

TIP

Because this is going to be included in your book, you might not want to include your address at the bottom of each page. However, don't overlook this valuable information when printing out Family Group Sheets to share with other researchers.

NOTE

The preparer name, address, and phone number will print at the bottom of the Family Group Sheet. However, the date will print at the top, opposite the title.

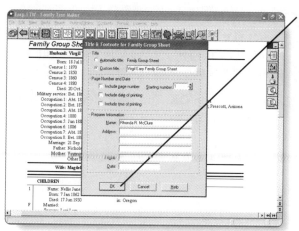

8. Click on **OK**. The Title & Footnote for Family Group Sheet dialog box will close and the changes will take effect on the Family Group Sheet Report that is displayed.

Using the Save View As Option

Once you have your report just the way you want it, you can save the report and use it later on in any of your books.

1. Click on **File**. The File menu will appear.

2. Click on **Save Family Group Sheet As**. The Save View As dialog box will open.

NOTE

This File menu option will change according to the report you have open.

3. **Type** the **name** of the report if you do not like the default name. The default name will be changed for the title that appears in the View list.

4. **Click** on **OK**. The Save View As dialog box will close.

TIP

You can always make changes to any saved view. The Open Saved View option in the File menu reopens the view, allowing you to make the changes.

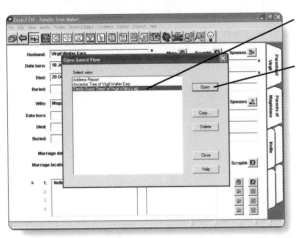

5. **Click** on the appropriate **view**. The view will be highlighted.

6. **Click** on the **Open button**. The Open Saved View dialog box will close and the selected Report view will open.

Renaming Outline Items

While Family Tree Maker has default names for all of the reports, you are not required to use those titles.

1. Click on **Books**. The Books menu will appear.

2. Click on **Open Book**. The Open Book dialog box will open.

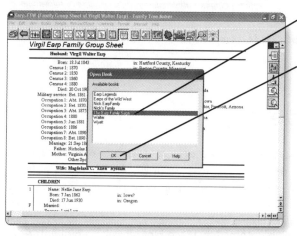

3. Click on the appropriate **book**. The book will be highlighted.

4. Click on **OK**. The Open Book dialog box will close and the Book view will open.

5. Click on the appropriate **item** in the Outline for list. The item will be highlighted.

6. Click on the **Properties button**. The Item Properties dialog box will open.

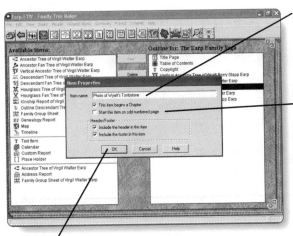

7. **Type** the new **name** in the Item name field. This will replace the old item name.

TIP

You can also set up chapter beginnings and control whether or not the report begins on an odd-numbered page. If the report is going to begin a new chapter, you might want to think about beginning that chapter on an odd-numbered page, which is the standard in most books.

---

8. **Click** on **OK**. The Item Properties dialog box will close and the item name will change in the Outline for list.

Adding Place Holders

Many times you will want to incorporate a family story created in another program, or some special hand-drawn charts or photo pages in your book. The place holder allows you to reserve a set number of pages anywhere in your book to insert these other items after printing.

1. **Click** on **Place Holder** in the Available items list. Place Holder will be highlighted.

2. **Click** on the **Add> button**. The Place Holder Properties dialog box will open.

3. Type the **name** of the item in the Item name field. The words "Place Holder" will be replaced with the name you have typed.

TIP

You will want to give the place holder a descriptive name so that you can easily recall what will go into those pages. This item name will be displayed in the Outline for list and, unlike in the other reports, you cannot open this item to refresh your memory about what is in it.

4. Click on the **up or down arrows** to select the number of pages to hold.

5. Click on **OK**. The Place Holder Properties dialog box will close.

6. Click on the **place holder item** in the Outline for list. The place holder item will be highlighted.

7a. Click on the **Move up button**. The place holder item will be moved up in the Outline for list.

OR

7b. Click on the **Move down button**. The place holder item will be moved down in the Outline for list.

> ### NOTE
>
> Don't forget that the Index must be the last item in the Outline for list. In fact, if you try to move something below it, Family Tree Maker will open a message box explaining that you cannot do that.

Adding to a Book

While you may have already created a book and saved it, this does not mean you can't build on that book. Family Tree Maker allows you to add additional reports at a later date to any previously saved book.

Adding Saved Reports to Books

You can incorporate Save View As reports into any book at any time. Once you have created them, they are available in any Books view, new or previously saved.

1. **Click** on **Books**. The Books menu will appear.

2. **Click** on **Open Book**. The Open Book dialog box will open.

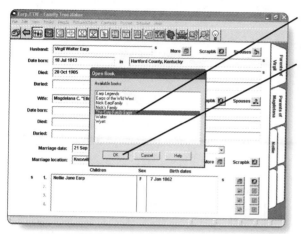

3. Click on the appropriate **book**. The book will be highlighted.

4. Click on **OK**. The Open Book dialog box will close and the Book view will open.

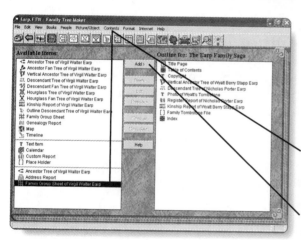

NOTE

The previously saved reports will always appear at the bottom of the Available items list.

5. Click on the appropriate **saved report** from the Available items list. The report will be highlighted.

6. Click on the **Add> button**. The report will be added to the Outline for list.

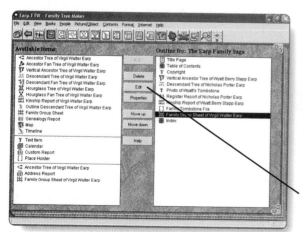

NOTE

At this point, the saved report can be repositioned or edited like the other items in the Outline for list.

7. Click on the **report**. The report will be selected.

8. Click on the **Edit button**. The report will open for editing.

9. Click on the **Go Back button** when you are done editing the report. You will be returned to the Books view.

> ### NOTE
>
> You can see the page number that has been assigned based on where the report is presently in the order of the book. This number will change if the report is moved up or down in the Outline for list in the Books view.

Adding Reports about Other Individuals

When a book is first created, it relies on the reports of the selected individual. Once a book has been saved, though, you can add additional reports about other people, giving you a lot of flexibility in your book and its layout.

1. Press the **F2 key**. The Index of Individuals dialog box will open.

2. Click on the desired **individual**. The individual will be highlighted.

3. Click on **OK**. The Index of Individuals dialog box will close and the Available items list in the Books view will reflect the change in individuals.

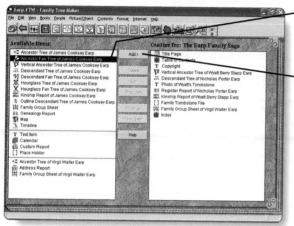

4. Click on the appropriate **item** in the Available items list. That item will be highlighted.

5. Click on the **Add> button**. The selected item will be added to the bottom of the Outline for list, just above the Index item.

TIP

If you click on the selected item in the Outline for list, you can use the various buttons to reposition the item, edit it, or change its properties. It is now a part of the book unless you elect to delete it.

NOTE

Notice that while you changed the focus of the individual in the Available items list, your saved reports are still available.

You have not only been introduced to Family Tree Maker, but you have been shown many of the advanced features and some tricks to get the most out of the program. Sharing your genealogy online or in print is limited only by your own possibilities. Happy ancestor hunting!

Part VI Review Questions

1. What happens when you change Beginning status of a marriage on the Family Page? *See "Getting Family Page and More About Marriage Facts to Work Together" in Chapter 20*

2. How do you remove a custom fact name that you created? *See "Removing a Custom Fact Name" in Chapter 20*

3. Can you export your Family File to a GEDCOM file? *See "Creating a GEDCOM File" in Chapter 21*

4. How do you open another Family File? *See "Opening a Different Family File" in Chapter 21*

5. What are four ways you can search for individuals to add to a Custom Report? *See "Using the Find Button to Include Individuals in the Custom Report" in Chapter 22*

6. Can you export the individuals from a Custom report in a GEDCOM file? *See "Saving as a New Family File or GEDCOM File" in Chapter 22*

7. Can you protect information on living individuals in your Family File? *See "Protecting Privacy" in Chapter 23*

8. How do you add another button to the toolbar in Family Tree Maker? *See "Customizing the Toolbar" in Chapter 23*

9. Can you create individual reports to include in your family history book? *See "Preparing Reports in Advance" in Chapter 24*

10. How do you add reports on a new person to a previously saved book? *See "Adding to a Book" in Chapter 24*

PART VII

Appendixes

A

Installing Family Tree Maker

Family Tree Maker has been designed to be easy to install. In this appendix, you'll learn how to:

- Install Family Tree Maker Version 10 on your computer
- Choose the options you want to install
- Uninstall Family Tree Maker from your computer

Installing Family Tree Maker Version 10

Most computers use an autorun feature when you put a new program CD into your CD-ROM drive—the CD begins to run without you having to do anything.

1. **Insert** the **Family Tree Maker 10 CD-ROM** into your computer's CD-ROM drive. The automatic installer will start.

NOTE

Family Tree Maker's installer will encourage you to close any programs you have running at the time you begin to install Family Tree Maker 10. (This is a good idea whenever you are installing software.)

---

2. **Click** on **Next** after you have closed all other open programs. The Access Your Online Data dialog box will open.

3. **Click** on **Next**. The Software License Agreement dialog box will open.

4. **Read** the **License Agreement**.

5. **Click** on **Yes**. The Choose Destination Location dialog box will open.

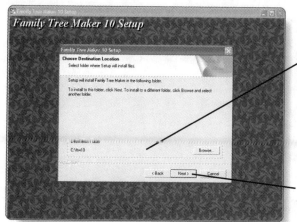

TIP

Usually the suggested Destination Folder is the most appropriate one. However, if you do not like where the installer is going to place Family Tree Maker, click on the Browse button and select another directory.

6. **Click** on **Next**. The Select Components dialog box will open.

Choosing Components

Family Tree Maker allows you to decide which of the available components you want to install.

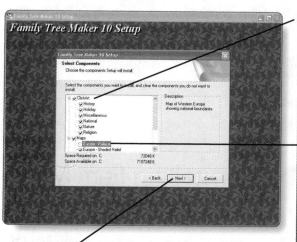

1. **Click** on the **check box** next to the components you want to install. A check mark will appear next to each component you select.

NOTE

By clicking on the ClickArt or Maps check box you automatically select all of the indented items under each heading. To exclude an item, click on the check box next to it to remove the check mark.

2. **Click** on **Next**. The Select Components dialog box will close and Family Tree Maker will begin to install.

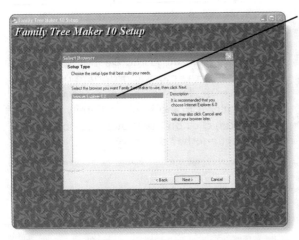

3. Select your **browser** and then **click** on **Next**. The final screen will appear.

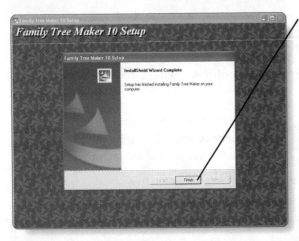

4. Click on the **Finish button** to complete the installation process.

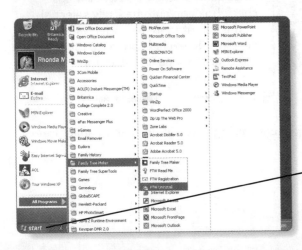

Uninstalling Family Tree Maker

There might come a time when you need to remove Family Tree Maker from your computer. Family Tree Maker has included an uninstall option.

1. Click on the **Start button**. The Start menu will appear.

2. **Move** the **mouse pointer** to All Programs. The Programs menu will appear.

3. **Move** the **mouse pointer** to Family Tree Maker. The Family Tree Maker menu will appear.

4. **Click** on **FTW Uninstall**. The InstallShield wizard will appear.

5. **Click** on **Remove**. The radio button will move to the Remove selection.

6. **Click** on **Next**. The InstallShield will verify you want to remove the program. Answering yes will remove the program. Answering no will cancel the InstallShield.

NOTE

On occasion you may find it necessary to reinstall the program if you are having problems. To do this make sure the radio button is next to Repair. When you wish to add clip art or maps that you did not install originally, select the Modify option to make these changes.

B

Using Keyboard Shortcuts

Many people prefer not to have to reach for the mouse when they're entering information. Keyboard shortcuts allow you to accomplish many of the tasks for which you would normally need to use the mouse. Throughout the book your attention has been called to some of the keyboard shortcuts included in this appendix, but here you can see the information at a glance. In this appendix, you'll learn how to:

- Use the keyboard shortcuts found in Family Tree Maker
- Use keyboard combinations in text windows

Learning the Keyboard Shortcuts

While it might seem like you will never remember the shortcuts, you will find that the shortcut commands become second nature as you spend more time in Family Tree Maker.

Getting Help

Although you can always open the Help menu, you can use the keyboard shortcuts shown in the following table to get to the help you need more quickly.

To execute this command	Do this
Use Family Tree Maker Help	Press the F1 key
Use the What's This? Button	Press the Shift and F1 keys at the same time (Shift+F1)

Working in Family Tree Maker

The following table puts the keyboard shortcuts related to Family Tree Maker commands together for an easy reference.

To execute this command	Do this
Create a new Family File	Press Ctrl+N
Open a different Family File	Press Ctrl+O
Print a report	Press Ctrl+P
Create a new To-Do item	Press Ctrl+T
Access the Index of Individuals	Press F2
View a source	Press Ctrl+S
Open the Other Spouses dialog box	Press F3
Access a More About Picture window	Press Ctrl+M
Get Family File status	Press Alt+F1
Get system information	Press Ctrl+F1
Exit Family Tree Maker	Press Alt+F4

Working with Text

While most of the entries in Family Tree Maker are made in fields, there are a number of text windows for typing notes. The following tables contain some shortcuts you might find useful when working in the text windows.

Selecting Text

The first step in manipulating your text is to select it. The following table offers some keyboard combinations for selecting a letter, a word, a line, or more.

To execute this command	Do this
Highlight the character to the right of the insertion point	Press Shift+ Right Arrow
Highlight the character to the left of the insertion point	Press Shift+Left Arrow
Highlight an entire word to the right of the insertion point	Press Ctrl+Shift+ Right Arrow
Highlight an entire word to the left of the insertion point	Press Ctrl+Shift+ Left Arrow
Highlight a line to the right of the insertion point	Press Shift+End
Highlight a line to the left of the insertion point	Press Shift+Home
Highlight a paragraph one line at a time	Press Shift+ Down Arrow for each line of the paragraph
Highlight all lines above the insertion point	Press Ctrl+Shift+Home

Copying and Pasting Text

After you select the text you want to work with, you might want to remove it or copy it for placement elsewhere. The following table contains the keyboard combinations you need to manipulate selected text.

To execute this command	Do this
Copy text	Press Ctrl+C
Cut text	Press Ctrl+X
Paste text	Press Ctrl+V
Delete text	Press Del

Glossary

Ahnentafel. German for *ancestor table*. In addition to being a chart, it also refers to a genealogical numbering system.

Ancestor. A person from whom one descends.

Ancestor Tree. Also known as a *Pedigree Chart,* this chart begins with a specific individual and displays direct lineage of all of the individual's ancestors.

Annotation. Personal notes or comments that either explain or critique. Family Tree Maker employs annotations in the Bibliography Report.

Bibliography. A report that shows a list of sources used to compile the information included in the genealogy. The sources follow an accepted format, which Family Tree Maker has built into the program.

BMP. Bitmap. A file format for graphics. Uses the .bmp file extension.

Book. In Family Tree Maker, a compilation of reports generated for a family or an individual, including family trees, miscellaneous reports, stories, photos, a table of contents, and an index.

Brightness. An adjustment that can be made to a scanned image to make the image lighter or darker.

Browser. See *Web Browser*.

Case Sensitive. Differentiating between uppercase and lowercase characters.

Citation. The accepted notation of the source of information.

Cite. The act of making note of the proof that supports a conclusion or claimed fact in the genealogy.

Clipboard. A memory feature of the Windows environment that allows a person to copy or cut text or graphics from one document and paste them into another.

Contrast. An adjustment made to a scanned image that causes the image to brighten or dim.

Cue Cards. The pop-up help windows that appear when you move from screen to screen in Family Tree Maker. They can be turned on or off using the system preferences.

Descendant. A person who descends lineally from another.

Descendant Tree. A chart that lists an individual and his or her descendants.

Endnotes. Source citations and explanatory notes that appear at the end of a document, specifically a tree or report.

Export. To transfer data from one computer to another or from one computer program to another.

Family File. Family Tree Maker's name for the database that contains the information about your lineage.

FamilyFinder Index. A genealogical list containing over 750 million names that is included in Family Tree Maker's CDs and online.

Family Group Sheet. A form that displays information on a single, complete family unit.

Family Page. The main screen in Family Tree Maker, into which you enter information about a particular individual and family.

Fastfields. Family Tree Maker remembers the names of the last 50 locations you have typed in so that as you begin to type in a place in a new location field, Family Tree Maker shows you possible matches based on the letters you have typed up to that point.

Format. One of Family Tree Maker's options for developing the style and look of reports and trees.

GEDCOM. GEnealogical Data COMmunication. A standard designed by the Family History Department of the Church of Jesus Christ of Latter-Day Saints for transferring data between different genealogy software packages. Uses the .ged file extension.

Genealogy Report. A narrative style report that details a family through one or more generations and includes basic facts about each member in addition to biographical information that was entered through Family Tree Maker.

Generation. The period of time between the birth of one group of individuals and the next—usually about 25 to 33 years.

GIF. Graphic Interchange Format. A graphic file format that is widely used in Web page documents. Uses the .gif file extension.

Given Name. The first name (and middle name) given to a child at birth or at his or her baptism. Also known as a *Christian name*.

Home Page. The main page of a Web site.

Hourglass Tree. A chart showing both the ancestors and the descendants of a selected individual. When printed, the tree resembles an hourglass because the ancestors spread out above the selected individual and the descendants spread out below.

HTML. Hypertext Markup Language. The standard language for creating and formatting Web pages.

Import. To bring into a program a file that was created using another program.

Individual Facts Card. A multi-tabbed dialog box that allows you easy access to all of the personal information (corresponding to the Family Page and More About pages) for a specific individual.

Inline Notes. The sources that appear within the text as opposed to at the bottom or end of a page in Family Tree Maker's Genealogy Reports.

JPEG. Joint Photographic Expert Group. Graphics that use the .jpg extension include a compression technique that reduces the size of the graphics file. Uses the .jpg file extension.

Kinship. In genealogy, this refers to the relationship between one individual and any or all of his or her relatives. This can be displayed through the Kinship Report in Family Tree Maker.

Maternal Ancestor. An ancestor on the mother's side of the family.

NGSQ. *National Genealogical Society Quarterly*. A periodical published by that society. Also refers to the NGS Quarterly numbering system offered in descending genealogy reports.

OLE. Object Linking and Embedding. A technology that allows you to create items in one program and place them in another, including video clips, still images, pictures, word-processing files, and spreadsheet files.

Outline Descendant Tree. A chart that shows in an indented outline format an individual's children, grandchildren, great-grandchildren, and so on through the generations.

Paternal Ancestor. An ancestor on the father's side of the family.

PDF. Portable Document Format. A file format that retains printer formatting so that when it is opened it looks as it would if on the printed page. Requires Adobe Acrobat

Reader to open and view a file that ends in the .PDF extension.

Pedigree Chart. A chart that shows the direct ancestors of an individual. Known in Family Tree Maker as an *Ancestor Tree*.

Preferred. A term Family Tree Maker uses in reference to parents, spouses, or duplicate events, meaning that you want to see that selection first or have it displayed in trees and reports.

Primary Individual. The main individual in any of the Family Tree Maker charts or reports.

Red-Eye Removal. The method of removing the red, or hollow, look of eyes from flash photographs that have been digitized.

Register. Refers to the descending genealogy format used by the New England Historic Genealogical Society. This also refers to their periodical by the same name.

Reports. Any of a number of standard and custom displays in various formats that Family Tree Maker can create.

Research Journal. A record used by genealogists to keep track of their research findings and tasks to be accomplished.

RTF. Rich Text Format. A cross-platform, cross-application text document format. It retains some of the formatting information that is supported by many word processors. Uses the .rtf file extension.

Saturation. The amount of color in each pixel of an image. When the saturation is high, the image shows bright, vivid colors. When the saturation is low, the picture may look black and white.

Scrapbooks. The term used by Family Tree Maker for the collections of photographs, images, video, sound, and OLE objects that can be stored for each individual and marriage in the Family File.

Siblings. Children of the same parents.

Source. The record, such as a book, an e-mail message, or an interview, from which specific information was obtained.

Spouse. The person to whom another person is married.

Surname. The family name or last name of an individual.

Threshold. As used in the Red-Eye Removal Dialog box, the minimum degree of redness for the pixels to be fixed.

Tree. The term Family Tree Maker uses to refer to its various charts. See *Ancestor Tree, Descendant Tree*, and *Outline Descendant Tree*.

URL. Uniform Resource Locator. The address used by a Web browser to locate a page on the Web.

WAV. Windows Audio Visual. The sound files that work with Media Player and Sound Recorder. Uses the .wav file extension.

Web Browser. The software that lets you access pages on the Web. The browser reads the HTML code and converts it to the pictures, colors, menu options, and overall design that you view on your monitor.

Web Page. A document on the Internet that is written using a scripting language such as HTML.

Web Site. A location on the Internet maintained by a single individual, company, or entity that provides information, graphics, and other items.

World Family Tree (WFT) Project. A multi-volume CD collection created by Genealogy.com from the genealogies submitted electronically by family history enthusiasts and indexed in the FamilyFinder Index.

World Wide Web. A graphical interface that is composed of Internet sites that provide researchers with access to documents and other files.

Index